The Constance Howard
book of stitches

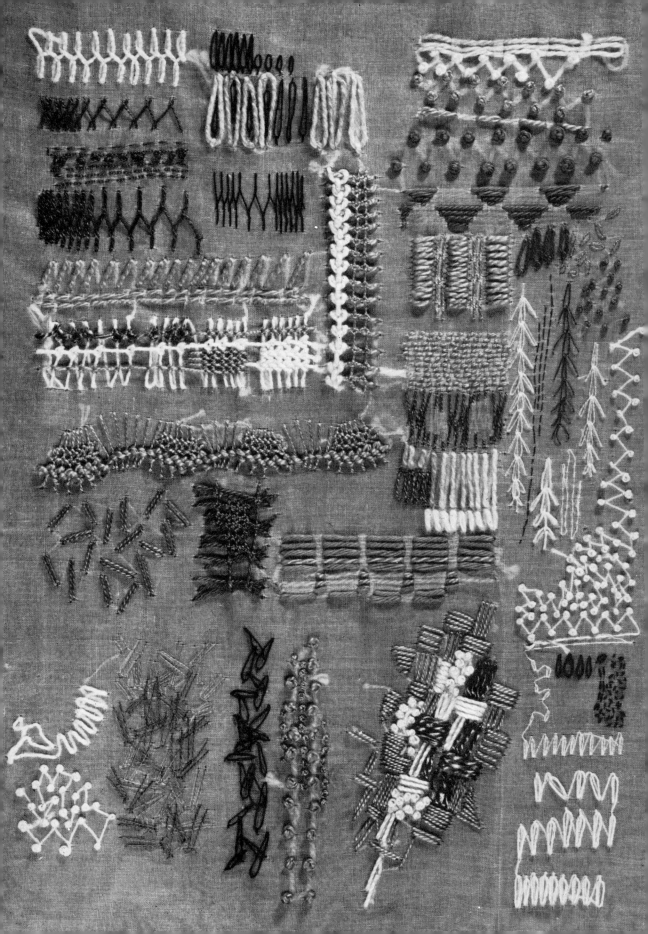

The
Constance Howard
book of stitches

B T Batsford Limited London

© Constance Howard 1979
First published 1979
Reprinted 1979, 1981
ISBN 0 7134 1005 1

Filmset in 'Monophoto' Bembo by
Servis Filmsetting Limited, Manchester
Printed in Great Britain by
The Anchor Press Limited, Tiptree, Essex
for the publishers
B T Batsford Limited
4 Fitzhardinge Street
London W1H 0AH

Contents

Acknowledgment 6

Preface 7

Captions to colour plates 8

Introduction 9
   Stitch choice; Tones; Texture; Threads;
   Needles; Techniques 10

Stitches
   Seeding 12
   Running 12
   Back and running 14
   Running and darning 14
   Stitching on hexagonal net 14
   Japanese darning 14
   Threaded running 18
   Pekinese 18
   Arrowhead 22
   Cross 24
   Stem 24
   Stem with chain at side 28
   Stem and variations 30
   Half Portuguese stem 30
   Stem with thread behind needle 30
   Stem and buttonhole 30
   Stem with twisted chain 30
   Double knot 32
   Double knot and variations 32
   Sorbello 34
   Stem variations, double knot, sorbello 34
   Sorbello variations 36
   Double knot and closed herringbone
     variations 38
   Buttonhole or blanket 40
   Crossed blanket 42
   Closed blanket 42
   Buttonhole and variations 42
   Loop 46
   Up and down buttonhole 48
   Knotted buttonhole 52
   Buttonhole 54
   Bonnet 56
   Feather 58
   Fly 58
   Twisted fly 62
   Fly variations 62

Sheaf 64
Sheaf filling 64
Herringbone 68
Herringbone and closed herringbone 68
Herringbone and variations 68
German interlaced herringbone 71
Herringbone pile 74
Knotted herringbone 76
Chevron 78
Cretan 82
Cretan and variations 82
Wave 86
Chain 88
Detached chain 88
Coral knot 92
Zigzag chain and variations 92
Zigzag coral 92
Twisted chain 92
Twisted chain 96
Double chain 98
Cable chain 98
Easy cable chain 98
Cable chain variations 98
Knotted cable chain variation 102
Stitch based on open chain 102
Rosette chain 104
Variations on twisted chain 106
Open chain 108
Heavy chain 108
Broad chain 110
Solid fillings 110
Wheatear 110
French knots 114
Bullion knots 114
Couching 118
Roumanian 120
Thorn 124
Raised chain band 126
Portuguese border 126
Raised stem band 126
Satin 130
Stitches on hexagonal net 132
Detached loop and variations 134

Suppliers 137

Index to stitches 139

Acknowledgment

This book of stitches is the result of a joint effort on the part of a group of excellent, enthusiastic workers, and Mabel Huggins and myself. The idea occurred in the middle of the night and when I was discussing it she felt that there were a number of embroiderers in the Tunbridge Wells Embroiderers' Guild who could produce practical work to make such a book possible. I felt that the subject as treated could become a useful reference book for embroiderers, however advanced, so Mabel Huggins organised a group of workers, who have produced a most exciting collection of samplers, from which it is obvious that they have enjoyed the work as much as I have enjoyed seeing the results. Mabel Huggins has contributed a number of super samplers to the book as well as organising the group. All of them have enjoyed the work and say that they have learnt a great deal in the process as each member solved her own interpretation of the stitches she had chosen. If these were unsuccessful she reworked the sampler.

I wish to thank everyone in the group and particularly Mabel Huggins who has devoted a great deal of time and thought to the work. I would also like to thank Trevor Grey for the excellent photographs. Molly Picken who knows what is required in the diagrams of stitches, always produces excellent drawings, for which I would like to thank her. Lastly, I really appreciate the support of Thelma M Nye of Batsfords who is always helpful and has encouraged us to compile the book.

C H *Chiswick 1978*

Those who worked the samplers are:

Bridget Barber	Crowborough
Clarice Blakey	Tunbridge Wells
Janet Grey	West Malling
Mabel Huggins	Tunbridge Wells
Annette Lane	Crowborough
Bridget Moss	East Peckham
Gwyn Skae	Wadhurst
Anne Wernham	Tunbridge Wells
Margaret Wood	Tonbridge

All members of the Tunbridge Wells and District Affiliated Branch of the Embroiderers' Guild.

Preface

The stitch as such probably evolved very slowly. It was first made with sinew, gut or grasses and used to fasten skins together by threading through holes punched with pieces of flint, bone, ivory or thorns. Crude oversewing repeated in an opposite direction would have produced cross stitches, while stab stitching may have resulted in double running. Gradually, rhythmic movements began to develop into stitches which could be remembered. An innate desire to decorate ourselves and our surroundings may have led to experiments, making loops, knots and threadings in grasses and other media which showed potential for pattern making as well as being used in securing skins to one another. Later, felt and cloth were sewn with spun threads and stitches developed into what is now embroidery.

Stitches as known were handed down from generation to generation, family to family, the repertoire being added to by travellers returning from foreign countries. They were invented by accident or intent, gradually becoming an international language, the same basic stitches being found in many parts of the world and in different countries. Today embroidery is open for experiment and stitches are a means of expressing original ideas in a lively, personal way.

In this book the idea has been to show some of the enormous scope of stitches, their versatility, the fascinating textures and patterns obtainable with them and the variety that is possible in working a stitch in different threads, changing its scale and spacing, working carefully, working freely, combining stitches to make new ones or altering the angle of the needle entering the fabric to vary the stitch. These have all been experimental approaches and it is hoped that from these results the reader will be inspired to try out more ideas for herself and to use them when appropriate.

Where the working of a stitch is obvious from the sampler, no diagram is given.

Straight stitch   *Trees   plate 1   facing page 48*
Fancy yarn, raffine, soft cotton, wool
In 1 strand of stranded cotton plus a slightly heavier twisted rayon.
Silk could be used. Stitches are isolated and overlap to give interesting
colour and texture

Raised chain band   *plate 2   facing page 49*
See also jacket

Laid work   *plate 3   facing page 72*
(a)   Roumanian over two threads in groups, number 3 perle cotton
(b)   Crosses over number 3 perle cotton in number 3 perle cotton and
     1 strand of stranded cotton
(c)   Roumanian couching, rayon over crochet cotton
(d)   Detached chain in soft cotton, coton-a-broder number 16 and
     perle cotton number 8, over number 5 perle cotton
(e)   Freely worked straight stitches in number 5 perle cotton over
     similar threads
(f)   Bullion knots over weaving yarns in number 3 perle cotton,
     coton-a-broder and stranded cotton
(g)   Detached chain in fine rayon and weaving yarn over weaving
     yarns

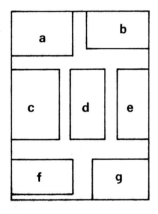

Stem stitch   *plate 4   facing page 73*
This sample employs a great variety of threads, from sewing cotton,
fine crochet cotton, rayon, nylon in several colours for the vertical
stitches, perle cotton number 8, raffine, slub cotton and gimp among
others

Introduction

Stitch choice

An idea can be emphasised by the right choice of stitch or stitches, a line, a band, a spot may be varied by the stitch selected, as may a rough, smooth or broken surface texture. Stitches may be flat, raised, looped or knotted. Two or even three may be combined to make a new one, using one thread or more for this operation, which gives a richer result, more knotty or raised or a heavier line. Some invented stitches are included here, such as stem with twisted chain added, stem with buttonhole. You can invent your own according to what you require.

Tones

There are particular qualities in embroidery that should be exploited. With stitches the direction in which they are worked can produce a great variety of tones, using one colour only. Satin stitches worked closely, in blocks, diagonally, horizontally or vertically will change according to direction, some blocks looking lighter than the original colour, some darker. Chain or stem stitch worked in close spirals so that sometimes the stitches are upside down show strong tonal changes. Raised stitches and looped stitches such as raised chain band, french knots, detached loops and double knot stitch cast shadows which affect the colour. Stitches variably spaced but joined such as cretan, ebbing and flowing as it were will change in tone value. Another way of giving variety of tone to one colour is to work with stranded cotton, using one thread gradually adding another and another until all six threads are being used for the same stitch. These experiments can lead to interesting design problems.

Texture

Interesting surfaces can be obtained by working with different textures of thread as well as by changing the direction of stitch. Perle cotton with wool, soft cotton with silk, hairy threads with smooth, heavy weights of thread with light are possible combinations. The tension in working a stitch can be tight or loose and planned deliberately affects the texture, so that stitches are sometimes integrated with the fabric, or are sometimes left very loose lying on the surface. There is a difference between conscious change of tension and badly worked stitches; between those freely interpreted and those carelessly handled. With a little practice this difference will be understood.

Threads

The article to be embroidered determines to some extent the choice of material or materials and sometimes a particular technique. This in turn may limit the stitches to be used, also the threads. A stitch is very much influenced by the type of thread selected, its weight, texture and colour, the same stitch worked in a smooth, fine thread looking quite different if worked in a heavy, fuzzy one. For example, stem stitch worked in one strand of stranded cotton, with long stitches in closely packed lines, makes a good all over texture, but worked in a heavy thread with shorter, more diagonally placed stitches, a rope like line results. Uneven running stitches in a fine thread, placed in rows close together give an interesting background effect but worked evenly with short stitches and equal spacing, in a coarse thread the appearance is bead like. With a fine thread, blanket or buttonhole stitch spaced apart and worked rather at random in interlocking rows of uneven size, gives a lacy quality or a mesh like structure. Worked in a heavier thread, with even stitches placed closely together a solid, fabric like structure results. Cretan and herringbone stitches are effective when worked freely in fine threads. They can be stitched over, superimposing different colours and textures to give interesting, broad bands, or interlocked, as a surface textures for larger areas. Knotted stitches are more effective in heavier yarns although they can be worked finely in thin thread for delicate fabrics, for example on a transparent one. French knots in soft thick cotton worked so that the connecting stitches between the knots show through from the back of the fabric give quite fascinating patterns. Fine threads are effective too, but a rich braid like result requires heavy yarn.

Try out stitches in different weights and textures of thread as some look better worked finely, some coarsely. Threads such as slub cottons should be couched, or may be worked over bars, and sometimes may be pulled through an open weave fabric. (Chenille, metal threads and some fancy weaving yarns) Stitches such as raised chain and raised stem band are possible using these threads if the bars are worked in fairly smooth non-stretchy thread. Mohair, angora and fuzzy threads are pleasant to use and give soft effects but avoid pulling them too many times through fabric as the fuzz flattens down. Stiff threads such as linen, nylon string, raffine and even nylon fishing line make stitches that tend to lie on the surface of the fabric, but are good for firm knotted and looped lace stitches and braid effects. Fine wools or mixtures, stranded cottons and pure silk threads merge well with soft fabrics such as woollens and woollen mixtures. Pile fabrics such as velvets and velveteens require stitches to show against the nap to be effective. When embroidery threads are difficult to obtain search around shops and stores for knitting and crochet yarns; synthetics, those mixed with lurex, oddments and natural coloured yarns that will dye are all useful. Threads used for stitches illustrated may be unobtainable in some areas but this does not matter as long as the weights are suitable and you do not find them difficult to handle.

Needles
The correct needles are important for good work. The eye of the needle should take the thread easily and doubled should pass through the fabric without a tug of war. If this happens it is usually the needle that is at fault and a larger one should be substituted. Special needles are obtainable for embroidery; chenille and crewel needles have points, oval eyes and short stems, chenille eyes being longer, crewel eyes slightly wider but shorter. They are obtainable in several sizes. Tapestry needles have blunt ends, long oval eyes and are used for counted thread work as they do not split the threads of the fabric. The eye of a pointed needle can be used if a tapestry needle is not available to push the thread through the fabric.

Techniques
It will be realised, if you have read so far, that most stitches are very versatile and that threads, needles and fabrics play a large part in their interpretation. They can be worked carefully and regularly, freely, larger or smaller than usual, they can be combined to form new stitches. The direction in which the needle is inserted into the fabric, horizontally, at an angle or vertically can change the appearance of a stitch; the spacing of one stitch with the next also affects this, stem stitch looking like a thin line or having a thick, rope like quality according to the proximity of each stitch and the angle at which the needle is inserted. Cretan stitch can be worked openly and

regularly as a band, closely, with stitches from short to long for a spot, or diagonally to give cloud like effects. The position of the cross over can be changed to give a diagonal line of pattern.

The amount of fabric taken up in the needle gives variety to the appearance of cretan stitch and also affects other stitches when the spacing changes. Herringbone is almost as versatile as cretan, worked freely, worked carefully, close together, varied in size, detached. Try out other stitches to see what happens to them.

Some stitches are more suitable for curves, others for straight lines or angles. Those that can diminish in size at top or bottom such as cretan, herringbone and blanket or buttonhole stitch are good for circles and with a little manipulation will will fit right angles, but very acute angles are difficult worked with broad stitches, lines being more easily fitted into points.

The preference for working all embroidery in a frame is a personal choice. Obviously some methods and some stitches are better when carried out on taut fabric. Metal thread embroidery, couching down threads, bead work, counted thread work such as needleweaving and drawn thread work and stitches such as satin and long and short, and those worked over bars are generally more efficiently carried out in a frame. Looped stitches such as buttonhole, cretan and chain are more easily worked if the fabric is not too tightly stretched or can be held loosely in the hand.

Before working freely it is necessary to know a few basic stitches from which others are developed. Play around with these with different kinds of yarn, on different background fabrics. Some that can be combined with other stitches or are a basis for invented ones are running stitch, buttonhole or blanket stitch, herringbone and twisted chain. Threads may be tied down by any means that are suitable or tied in knots of different sizes and couched down with suitable stitches. By using both fabrics and threads as you wish, you will discover your own means of combining stitches, of inventing new ones, discarding those that do not express what you want. You will find it difficult to stop once started.

Stitches

Sampler *frontispiece*
Worked at random. Included are: french knots, satin, raised chain band, detached chain, running, wheatear, fly stitch, cretan, seeding. A variety of threads is used for the sampler, soft cotton, perle cotton numbers 3, 5 and 8, stranded cotton

Seeding
Consists of random small back stitches, worked very closely or scattered. The stitch is sometimes called *speckling*. It can be a basis of interesting colour combinations

Running *opposite*
Running on the counted thread
Random running on the curves
Running leaving loops of thread loose on the surface
The weight of thread creates different effects
Wool, soft cotton, stranded cotton, perle cotton numbers 5 and 8 in browns, golds and fawn on grey are used for the sampler

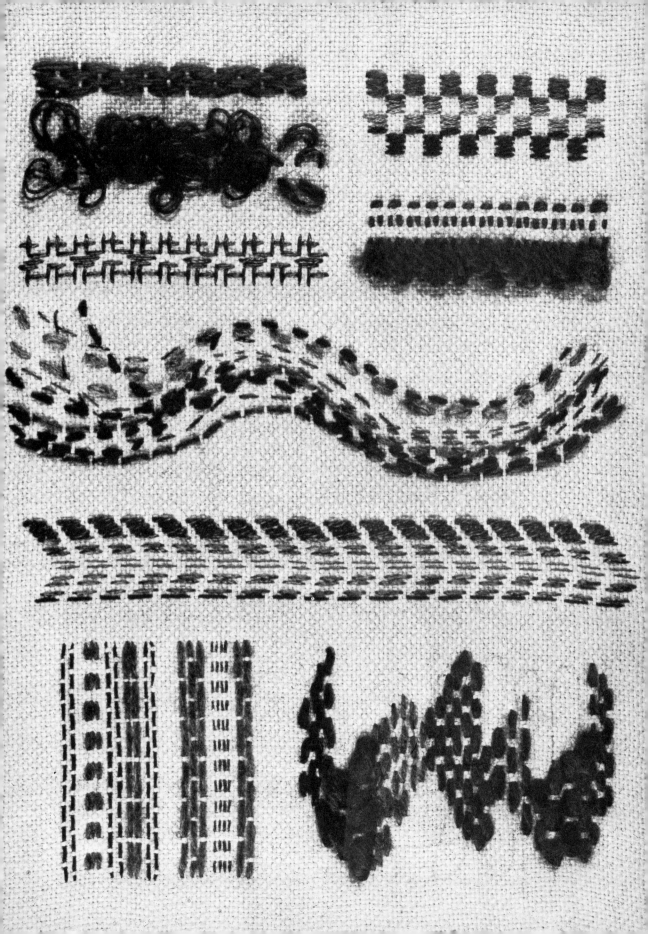

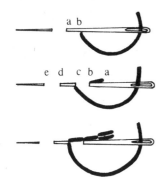

★ Back and running stitch

1 Work a running stitch (b–a) bringing the needle out for the next stitch at (c).
2 Go back into the first stitch (b) to make a back stitch, at the same time bringing the needle out at (c), in at (d) and out at (e), making a running stitch and back stitch.

Variation Work two back stitches instead of one to make a more knobbly line. Rows may be closely worked to produce solid areas of stitches.

★ See Jacqueline Enthoven, *The Stitches of Creative Embroidery*, Van Nostrand Reinhold, New York.

Back and running stitch *opposite*
In white and honey coloured yarns on a green background. Sometimes one back stitch is worked, sometimes two back stitches A variety of patterns may be made with this stitch, which is worked in soft cotton, perle number 5 and heavy crochet cotton.

Running and darning *overleaf*
The stitches are in white and cream on scarlet cotton. The pattern darning is worked by picking up threads of the fabric at definite intervals. The length of stitch and the spaces in between, the spacing of the rows of stitches and the use of fine to coarse threads in one pattern give great variety to the final effect. Perle cotton numbers 3, 5 and 8, 1 strand of stranded cotton, coton-a-broder number 16, slub cotton and rayon are employed

Stitching on hexagonal net *page 17*
The stitches are darned on the hexagonal net, to produce different lacy borders. They include herringbone, simulated Japanese darning, star stitch. Both sides of the stitches are visible so create a certain richness. Perle cotton number 8 and fine weaving yarns in white on white net, make an attractive sampler

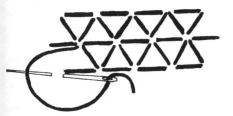

Japanese darning
Work the horizontal rows first, then connect these with the diagonal stitches. On the sampler the horizontal and diagonal stitches are worked in one operation

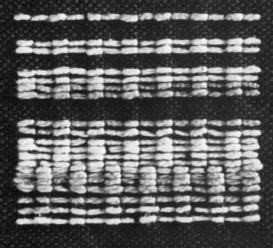
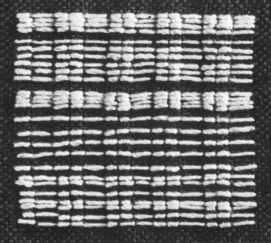
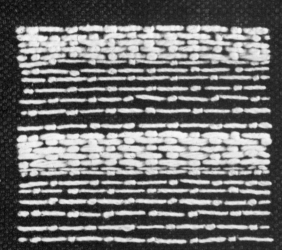
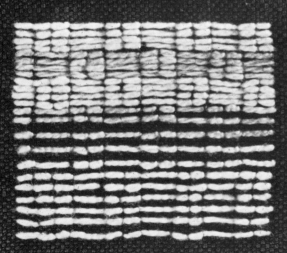

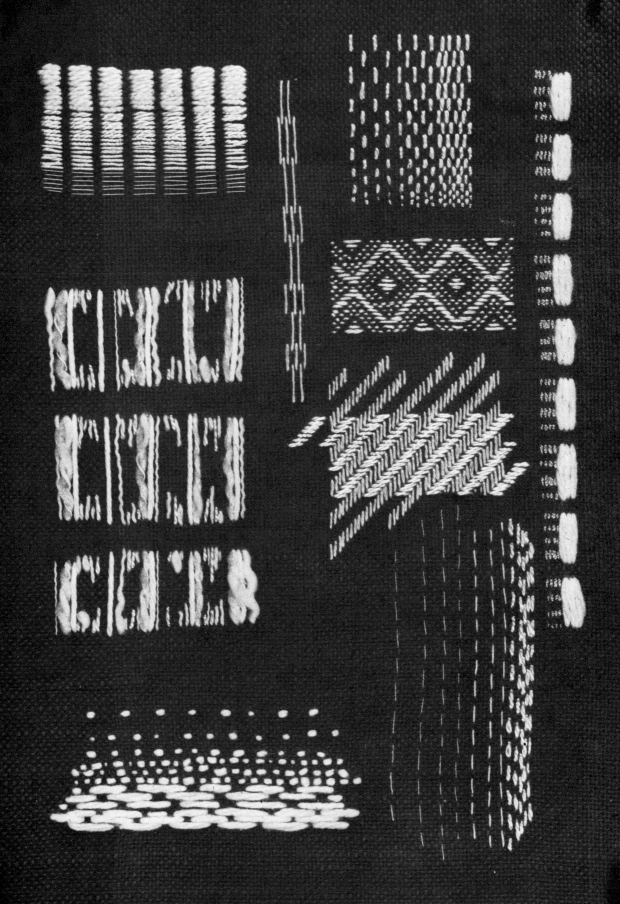

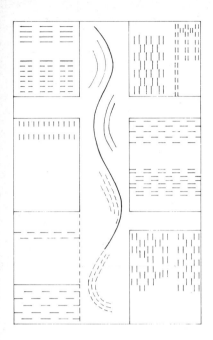

Threaded running *opposite*
This sample is in white stitching on a scarlet ground, using a variety of threads, such as fine and coarse wool with a matt texture, fine rayon crochet thread, heavier nylon, rayon and number 8 perle cotton
The back of the sampler has been drawn to show the structure of the running, on which the threaded patterns are built up

Threaded running *overleaf*
The threading is gimp, perle cotton number 3, nylon, rayon, raffine, weaving yarns, thick wool. The running is worked in a non-stretch thread, perle cotton numbers 5 and 8. The background is a charcoal linen with white, cream and grey stitches

Pekinese *page 21*
In the past, owing to its extreme fineness, working this stitch resulted in blindness for many Chinese embroiderers until it was banned, hence it was called 'the forbidden stitch'. A backstitch is worked from right to left and then is threaded from left to right. Thick, soft wool, soft cotton, rayon, fine untwisted silk, fine crochet cotton or rayon, perle cotton numbers 5 and 8, slub cotton and nylon are used for the stitches on this sampler, which are in white and cream on turquoise linen

18

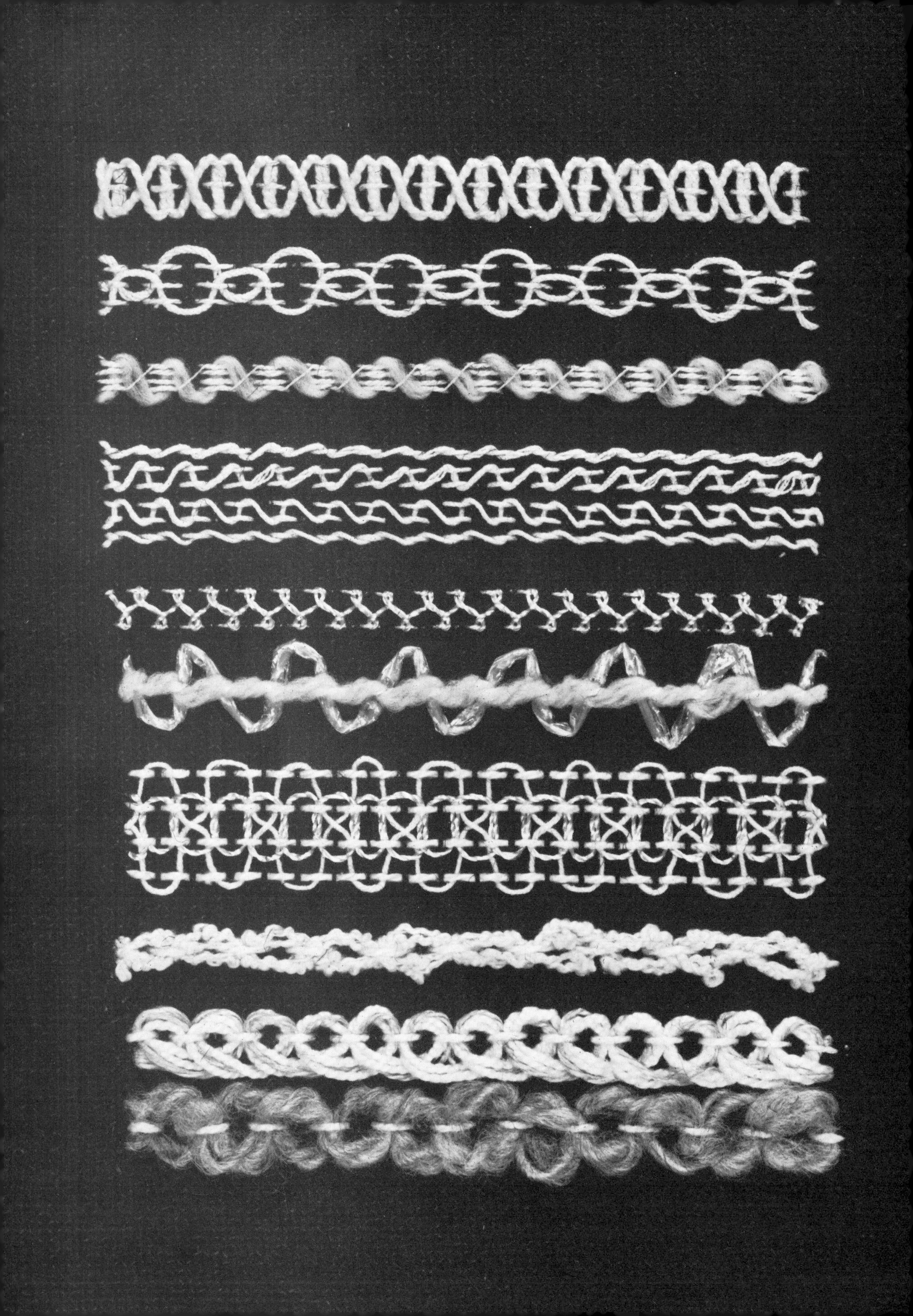

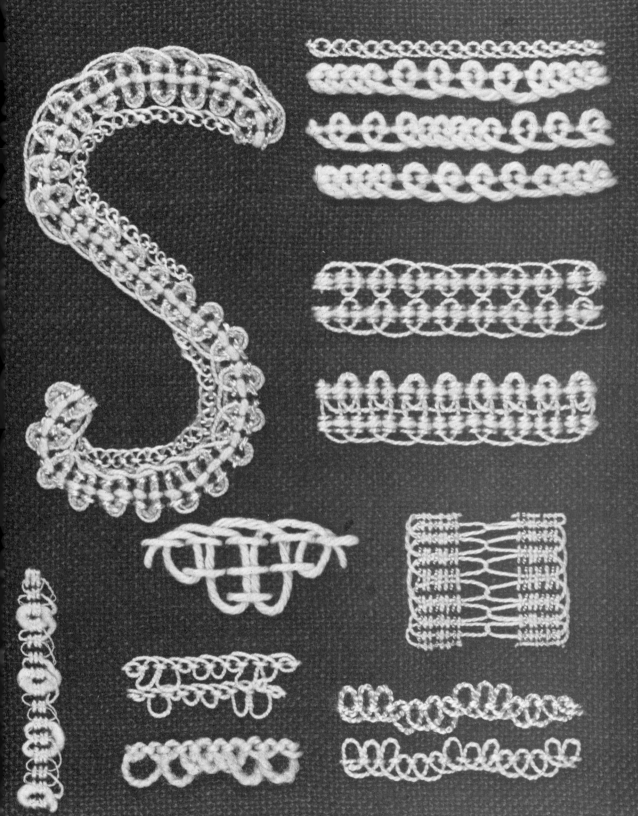

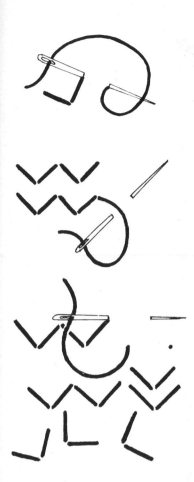

Arrow or arrowhead stitch

Stitches are worked at right angles to one another. The usual method is to work from left to right with slanting stitches, making two stitches on the wrong side on the upward movement. The same effect is obtained by working two parallel rows of back stitches on the wrong side of the work, with the zigzag on the right side; or by working one row of stitches, filling in on the return journey. The stitch may be worked also in pairs or vertically

Arrow or arrowhead stitch   *opposite*

Consisting of freely worked straight stitches sometimes detached, sometimes overlapping. The different weights of thread give the stitches variety and vitality. Weaving yarns, rayon, sewing cotton, perle cotton numbers 5 and 8 and wool in browns, golds and greys on pale grey linen are used for the stitches, which are arranged to give an appearance of upward growth

Cross stitch on linen   *opposite*
A free interpretation using a fine twisted cotton, rayon, several
weights of wool plus heavy slub wools in dark browns, mid browns
and golds on a grey background
This stitch is worked regularly on canvas or for counted thread
embroidery, smoothness being obtained by keeping both under and
upper stitches always in the same directions, eg the under one to the
right, the upper to the left.

Slanting stem

Alternating stem
or cable stitch

Stem stitch
Worked with the thread to the right of the needle. To the left of the
needle the stitch is called *outline*. The back of the work shows a line of
back stitch.
Work from left to right or upwards from the base. Very long stitches
worked in fine thread in lines close together give a good background
texture; with the horizontal stripe made where the stitches overlap
interesting patterns emerge. By alternating the thread to the left and
the right of the needle a brick-like effect is obtained. By slanting the
needle more diagonally a rope-like effect is obtained

Stem stitch   *overleaf*
Showing curved and straight lines. Worked in soft cotton, wool,
rayon, perle cotton numbers 5 and 8 and fine weaving yarn, on a pale
grey ground with stitches in black and brown

Stem stitch   *page 27*
In straight lines on a pale grey ground in black and various shades of
brown yarns
Stitches are in soft cotton, rayon, wool, perle cotton numbers 3 and 5
with some weaving yarn

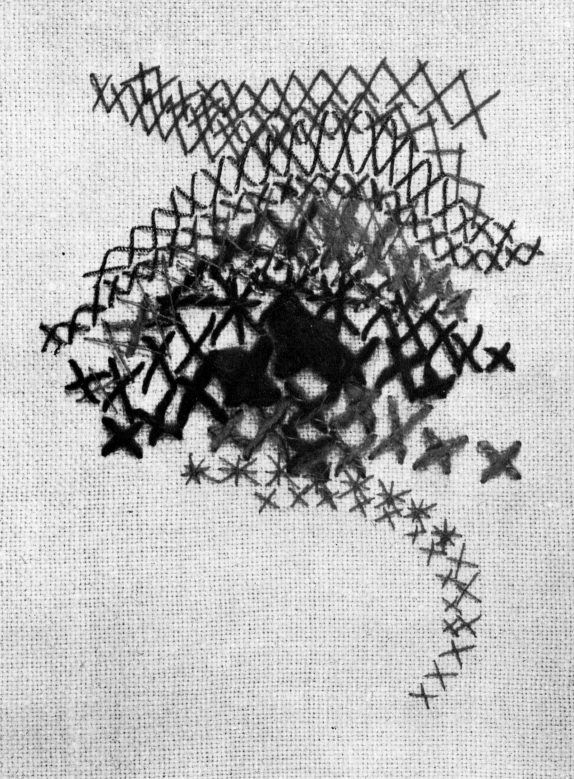

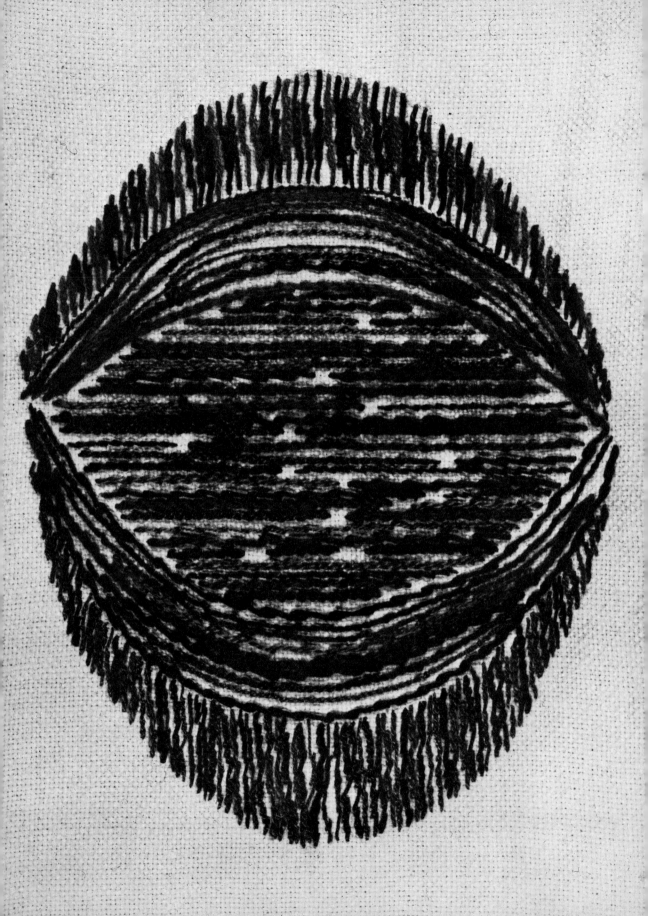

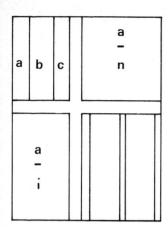

Stem variations *opposite*
Left block above and right block below
(a) Elongated stem in one strand of stranded cotton
(b) Raised stem band
(c) as (a)
The lower right block is repetitive

Upper right block
Variations on stem, combined with other stitches, worked horizontally. Reading from the top row and worked:
(a) from the left, stem with buttonhole in soft cotton, the thread pulled up
(b) the same with different yarn in perle number 8 worked from the right
(c) elongated stem in one strand of stranded cotton
(d) stem with buttonhole and chain stitch, worked from the right. Perle number 5. Needle pointing to the left for the buttonhole
(e) as (c)
(f) variation in soft cotton, as (a) worked from the right
(g) stem with chain in rayon, worked from the right
(h) wrapped stem – half Portugese, perle number 8 wrap the previous stitch once
(i) as (d) but worked from the left in soft cotton
(j) as (c)
(k) as (d) worked from the right in soft cotton
(l) as (c)
(m) as (g) in perle number 8
(n) wrapped with buttonhole – soft cotton and perle number 8

Lower left block
Worked upwards. From the left:
(a) 3 rows of wrapped stem, perle cotton number 8 and rayon
(b) elongated stem in one strand of stranded cotton
(c) stem and chain, perle cotton number 8 and rayon (2 rows)
(d) as (b)
(e) outline loop, perle cotton number 5 and 8 (2 rows) worked by turning fabric upside down, and from bottom to top
(f) as (b)
(g) stem variation with buttonhole, in rayon
(h) as (b)
(i) variation in perle number 5. Stem with buttonhole, with the thread pulled upwards

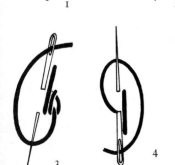

Stem with chain at side
Work stem, then take the needle to the left and work a chain, with (upside down) needle pointing upwards (1). Continue working stem with the chain on the left (2). The length of stem stitch gives variety to the effect. The chain may enter the point of each stem stitch, or it may be parallel with it as in (3) and (4)

28

Stem and variations – all stem – back stitch on back
Work stem and with the thread below the needle on the left, work a loop with the needle horizontal, continue to work stem with wrong side giving a back stitch, with a loop on each stitch, not through fabric

Half Portuguese stem
The stem is wrapped once, going through two stitches. The thread is kept above the needle which does not penetrate the fabric

Half Portuguese

Invented stitch   *page 31*
Based on stem with buttonhole. Work stem stitch, then work a buttonhole loop from left to right, across the stitch, with the needle entering the fabric at the top of the stem stitch, but coming out away from and halfway down the length of this stitch (1). Pull the needle thread upwards to produce the cross
Now take the needle back into the fabric to emerge by the stem stitch for the next one (2). The spaces between the crosses may be varied, short or long as required. The final result (3) gives a raised, twisted cord-like stitch

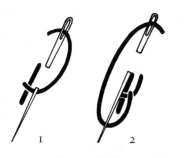

I   2

Stem with buttonhole

Stem with twisted chain or bullion   not worked on sampler, but gives an interesting result
Work a stem stitch and then with needle on the right side and the point down, work a twisted chain (1). If right handed twist thread over the needle: gives a plaited look. Continue with stem stitch (2), or work a bullion by twisting 5 or 6 times, according to the length of the stem stitch and half stem stitch

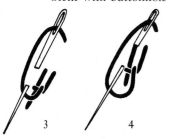

3   4

Variations

Stem with buttonhole
Work a stem, then work a buttonhole loop by the side on the right (1), the needle again can be taken by the side or through the top of the stem (2). Continue with stem and buttonhole.
Variation (3) work buttonhole on right, then on left and continue with stem and two buttonhole stitches.
Variation (4) work buttonhole on the right and chain on the left of the stem stitches.

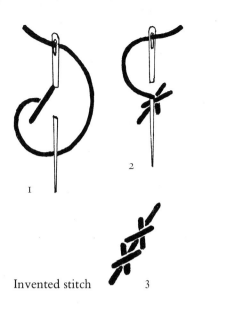

Invented stitch 3

Stem with
twisted chain

Stem with wrapped chain

This stitch depends on tension, a firm heavier thread is best used.
Work stem, take the thread behind the needle which is inserted parallel
on the right of the stitch point downwards, by the stem stitch but half
its length. Wind the thread round the point of the needle, and bring
the needle through the fabric, pulling thread tightly (1). Continue
with next stem (2)

Stem with wrapped chain

Stem with twisted chain and chain stitch

Use firm non-slippery thread
Work 2 stem stitches to give back stitches on the wrong side.
Work twisted chain through these two stitches, not through the
fabric (1).
Continue working twisted chain through two stem stitches. The
angle of the twisted chain stitch can produce variations in the
appearance of the stitch
Variation (2) Take the needle up through the last stem stitch and
through the tail of the twisted chain, then work a chain stitch round
the twisted chain, taking the needle through the fabric to hold the
stitch firm – tension is important here. The gap made between the
stitches is closed with the twisted chain. The angle of the chain stitch
should follow that of the twisted chain. Stitches should be fairly close
together for a really chunky result

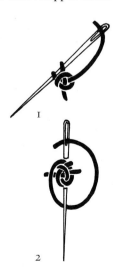

31

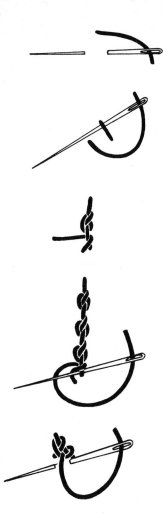

Double knot and variations

Looks like raised chain band, and can be worked as such, with wide basic stitches.

(a) Work double knot on the starting bar which is diagonal.
(b) Work buttonhole loops as in the diagram, one on the left and one on the right bars. These loops may be worked alternately on the left or right bars, or two or even three loops may be worked on the bars, provided these are sufficiently long.

Variations see the diagrams below

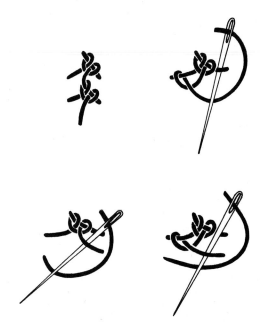

Double knot

Double knot variations

Double knot *opposite*

Sometimes called Palestrina and in structure similar to Sorbello stitch. It can give an appearance of beads and for a good effect is best worked in a thickish thread, such as perle cotton number 3 or 5. Work from left to right or vertically

Worked without variations in soft cotton, rayon, weaving yarns, fine wool, very fine cotton and perle cotton number 8. The background is greenish grey, the stitches are in white

32

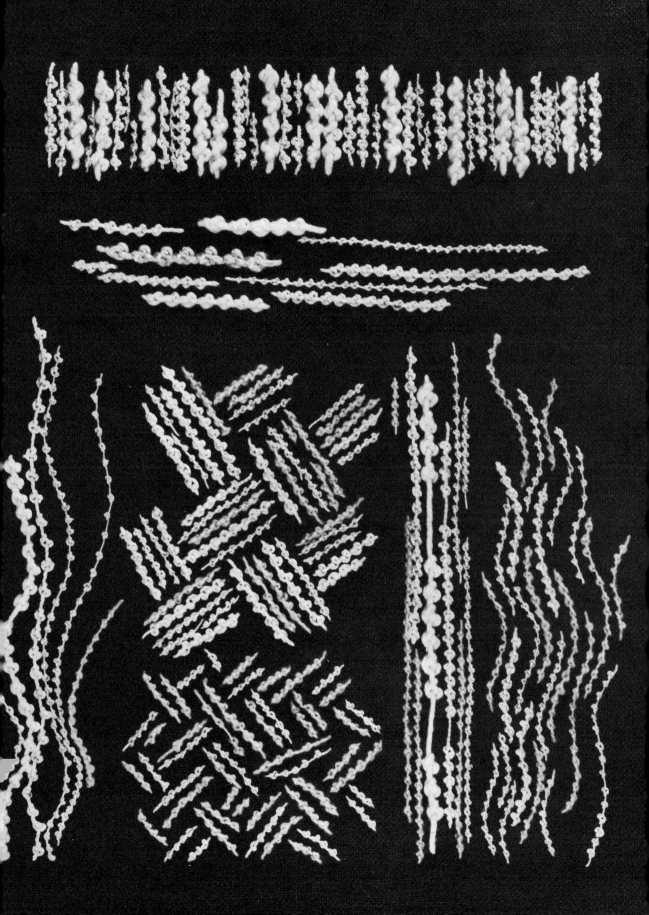

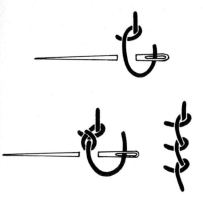

Sorbello

Sorbello is a knotted stitch which is worked horizontally, in rows or may be detached; or may be worked diagonally or vertically. Variations show each successive row of stitches interlocked into the previous one. Numerous other arrangements are possible

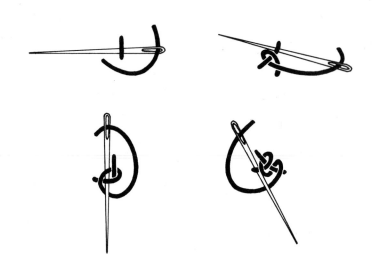

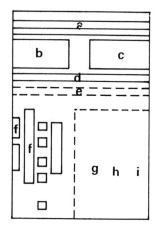

Stem stitch variations   double knot, Sorbello   *opposite*

(a) Double knot stitch worked from right to left further apart than usual. The second row is similar but starts from the opposite end

(b) A slight variation on sorbello stitch

(c) Sorbello

(d) An invented stitch derived from sorbello with twisted chain. Worked from the right side in the illustration

(e) Herringbone with double knot worked over each bar not through the fabric. In the sample the fabric has been turned round, the stitch starting from the left side

(f) Similar to (d), worked from the top to the bottom, fabric upside down. Read from the bottom

(g) Stem stitch with twisted chain worked through two stem stitches but not through the fabric

(h) Stem stitch with horizontal blanket or loop stitch. The blanket stitch wraps two stem stitches together but does not go through the fabric.

(i) Stem stitch with twisted chain, wrapped round with chain stitch, which is worked through the fabric to hold it. A slippery thread is unsuitable for this stitch.

The background is turquoise cloth with stitches in white and cream perle cotton numbers 3, 5 and 8, and soft cotton.

34

Sorbello variations

Work horizontally as for regular stitches but make the tail of the first stitch long, the second stitch short and tight.

Work vertically, starting with regular sorbello. Bring the needle below for the beginning of another square. Thread alternately through the outside loops of the previous stitch and the inside loops. One or more loops may be threaded on each of the previous ones, to make a thick braid like pattern. Use firm, thickish threads, or fine stiff ones for a lacy result.

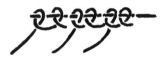

Sorbello with tails

Sorbello variations *opposite*

Crochet cotton, perle cotton numbers 3, 5 and 8, and soft cotton are used in white, fawn and dark brown on scarlet cotton fabric. The stitches are looped into the previous stitches, alternately once on the outside of the previous loops and within the loop, twice outside and twice or three times within the loop. The more loops on each of the previous stitches the heavier is the braid like appearance of the finished work.

36

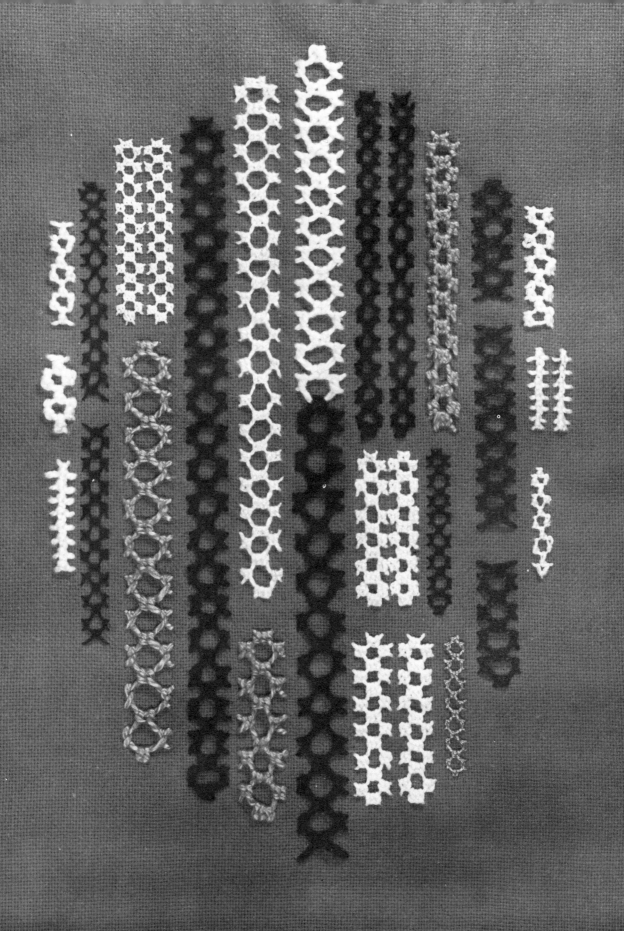

Double knot and closed herringbone variations *opposite*

From top

> Closed herringbone with twisted chain on one bar only, not through fabric. Crochet cotton
>
> Double knot worked from the left on the sampler, tie-dyed crochet cotton
>
> Closed herringbone with twisted chain on two bars, soft cotton
>
> Worked the opposite way round in perle number 5, tie-dyed
>
> Two rows of double knot stitch in crochet cotton
>
> Double knot in soft cotton
>
> Double knot with buttonhole on the left bar, perle cotton number 5, tie-dyed.
>
> Double knot with 2 buttonhole stitches on the left bar, soft cotton, perle number 5. The top one in soft cotton, the lower in crochet cotton
>
> Invented stitch in soft cotton
>
> Double knot stitch in perle number 8

Herringbone with
twisted chain variations

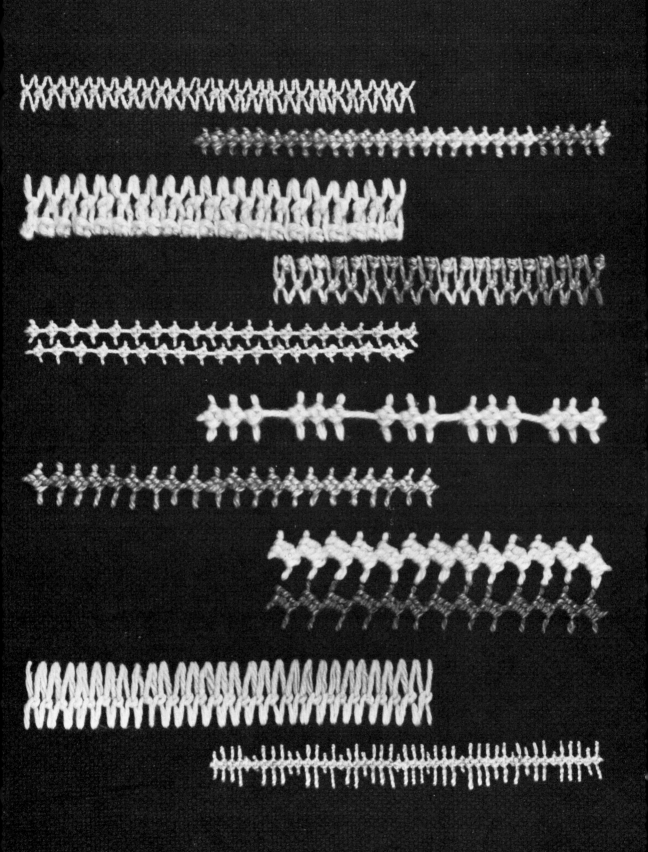

Buttonhole

variations

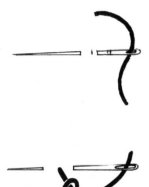

Buttonhole

Blanket stitch or buttonhole
A loop stitch with many variations, for example, straight loop stitch, a knotted variety, knotted buttonhole, up and down buttonhole. The samples show many different approaches with some fillings. If working with the right hand, twist the thread over the needle when working from left to right.

Buttonhole or blanket stitch   *opposite*
These stitches are worked in patterns similar to those found on an early sixteenth century Swiss embroidery of the Nativity, in the Victoria and Albert Museum, London. The background of this sampler is charcoal with white stitches in perle cotton numbers 5 and 8, coton-a-broder number 16 and soft cotton
Note the buttonhole structure on which the needleweaving is worked. Any stitches which are built up over bars could be worked on a buttonhole foundation. Examples that could be used are raised chain band, raised stem band, Portugese border. In this way strongly textured areas can be developed

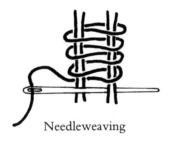

Needleweaving

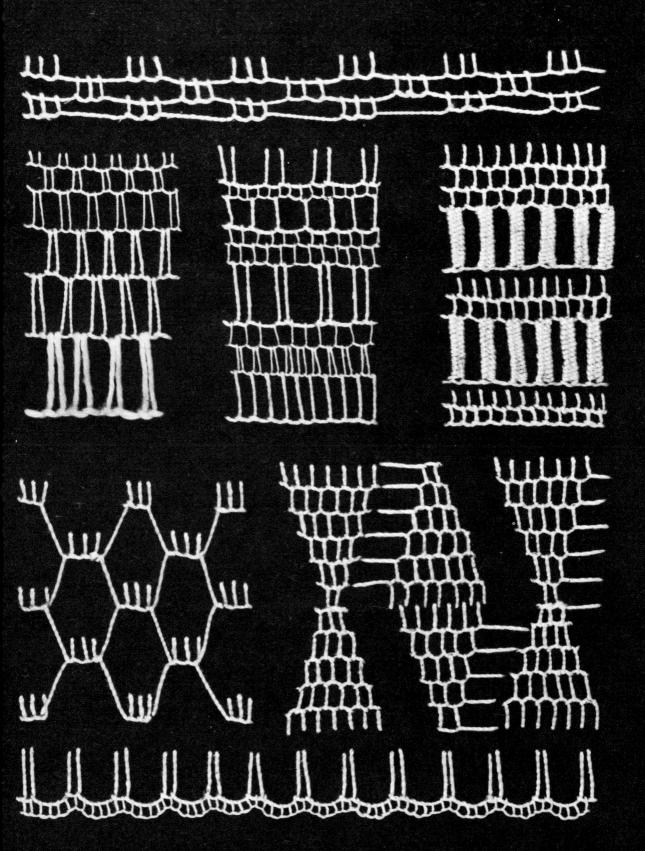

Crossed blanket stitch   *opposite*
White stitches on a greenish grey background are worked in slub cottons, fine wools, 1 strand of stranded cotton, perle cotton numbers 5 and 8, sewing cotton, soft cotton, rayon and weaving yarn

Crossed blanket

Closed blanket stitch   *overleaf*
Brown threads on a pale grey linen are worked in a variety of yarns from fine to coarse, sewing cotton, 1 strand of stranded cotton, fine wool, perle cotton numbers 5 and 8, and soft cotton

Buttonhole and variations   *page 45*
Cream and white threads on dull green are worked freely. Fine poodle wool, wool, slub cotton, 1 strand of stranded cotton, perle cotton numbers 5 and 8 and coton-a-broder are used for the stitches

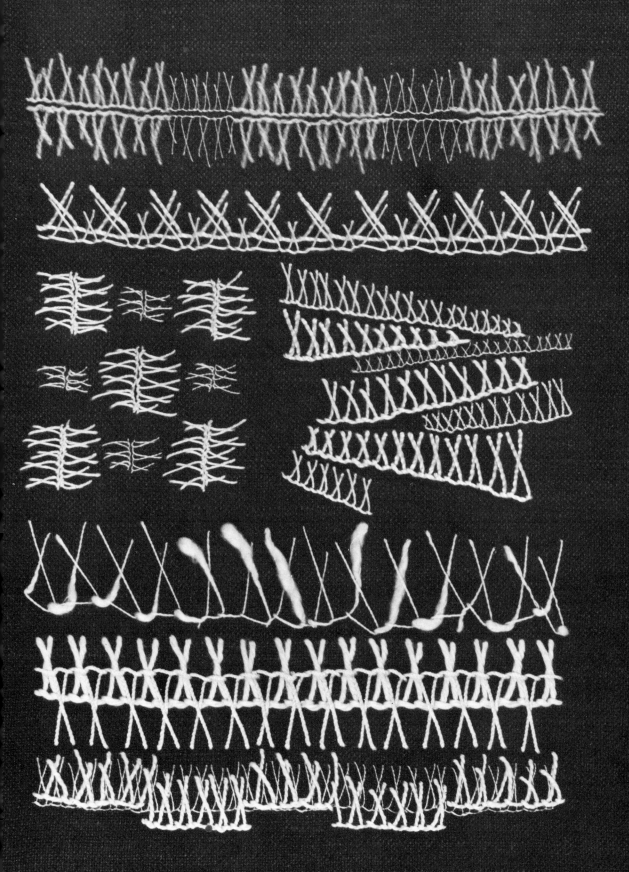

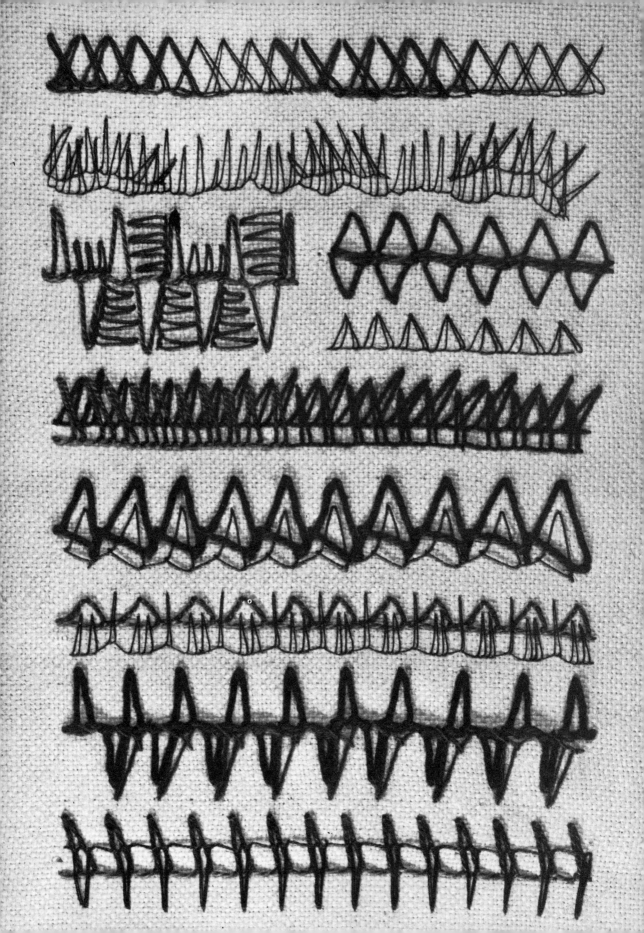

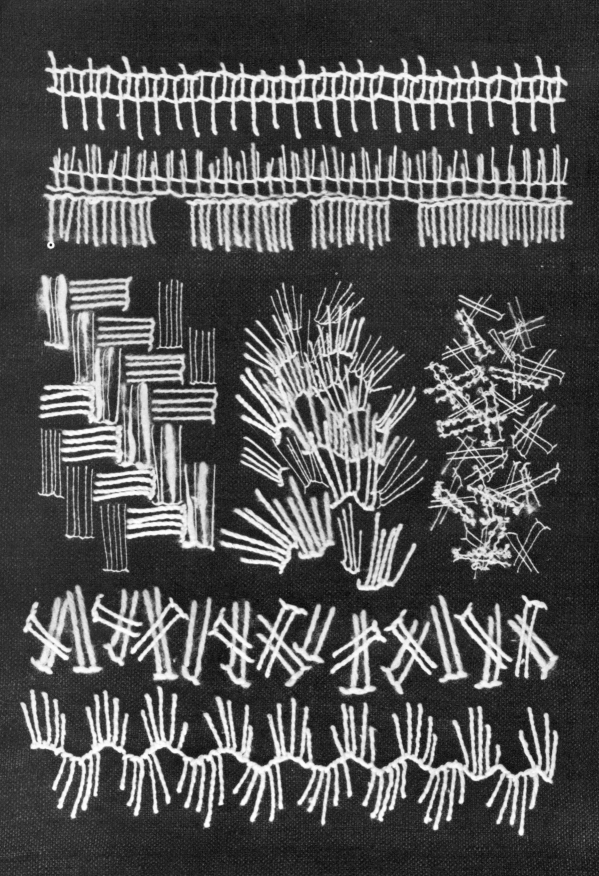

Loop stitch

Work from right to left. Bring needle through in centre of band. Insert needle a little to left of starting point at top of band and come through immediately below at bottom of band. Needle then loops the thread over the first stitch without passing through fabric as in diagram.

Length and angle of stitch can produce variations.

In curved shape, needle has twice entered same hole to produce points.

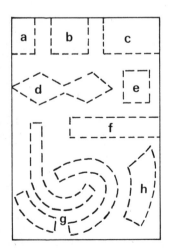

Loop stitch *opposite*
(a) Interlocked fine rayon
(b) Nylon and soft wool
(c) Nylon
(d) 1 strand of stranded cotton and number 8 perle cotton
(e) Number 5 perle cotton with 1 strand of stranded cotton
(f) Soft wool with fine gimp interlaced between the wool
(g) Nylon, twisted rayon, weaving yarn
(h) Fancy wool and weaving cotton
The sampler is worked in white on dark grey fabric

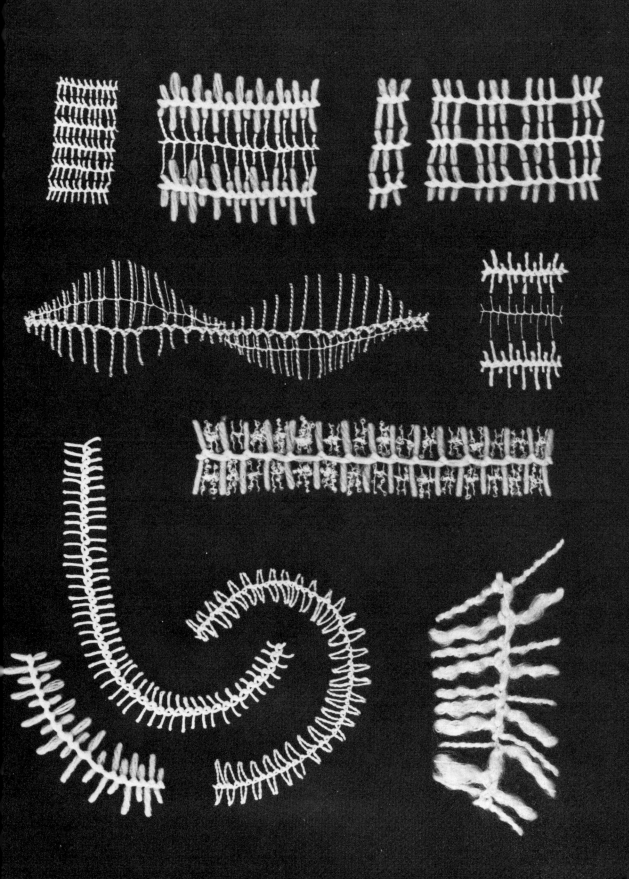

Up and down buttonhole *page 49*
Using a variety of weights of yarn, sewing cotton, fine wools, rayon, fancy weaving yarns, raffine, soft cotton, in white on blue fabric

Up and down buttonhole *page 50*
In white stitching on a brownish grey linen.
Raffine, coton-a-broder number 16, perle cotton number 5, fine wool, soft cotton and 1 strand of stranded cotton give variety to the results

Up and down buttonhole variations *page 51*
In white stitching on a brownish grey linen. As in number 22, a variety of yarns is used, including slub cotton, 1 thread of stranded cotton, perle cotton number 8, weaving yarn and crochet cotton

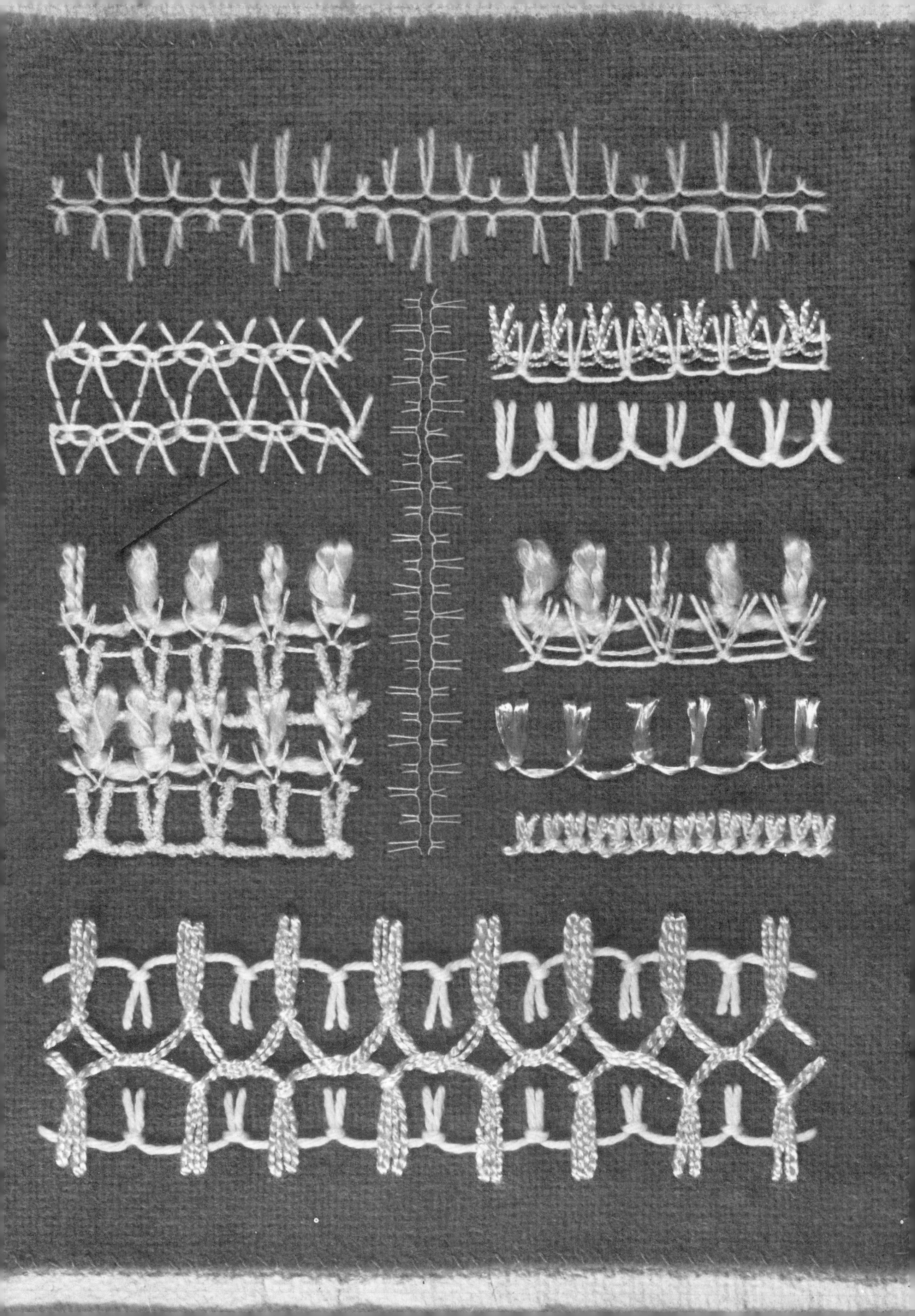

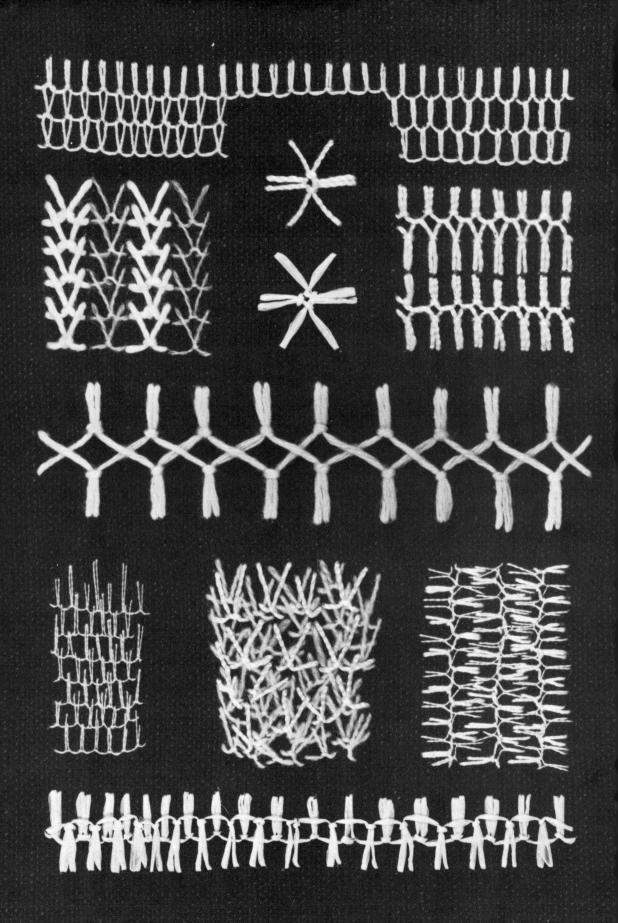

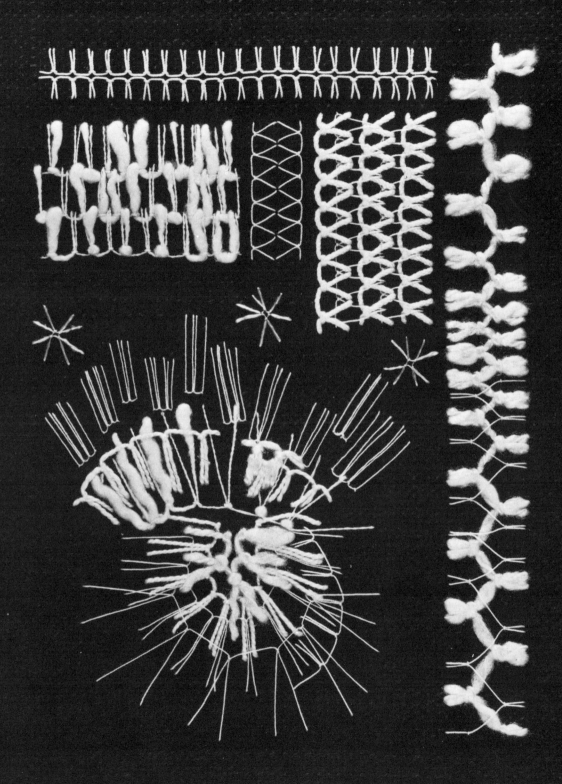

Knotted buttonhole *opposite*
Left to right worked as curved bands
     Soft cotton and fine crochet rayon
     Perle cotton number 8 and soft cotton
     Perle cotton number 8
     Soft cotton
     Perle cotton number 8
     Fine crochet rayon
The stitches are in white on charcoal fabric

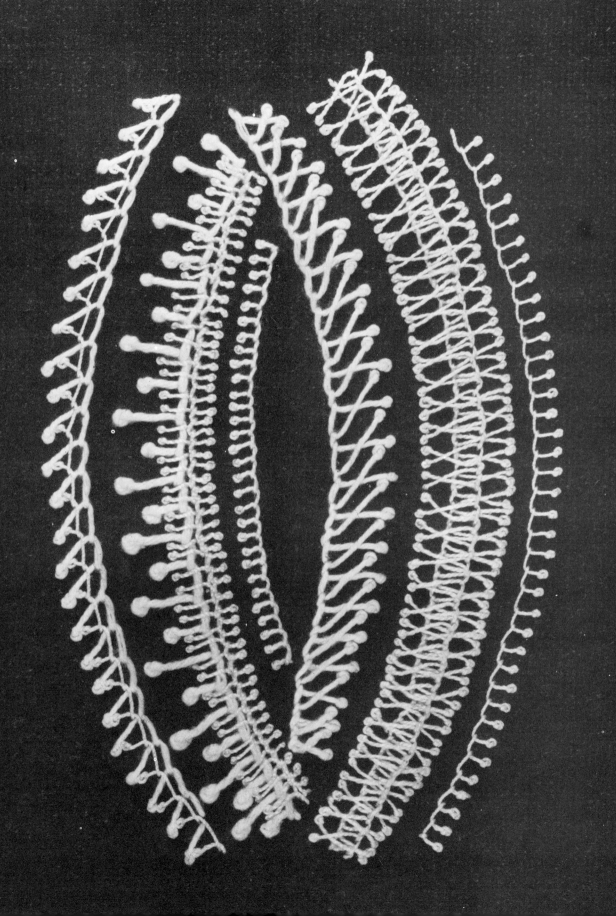

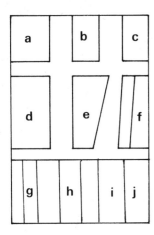

Buttonhole and needle weaving on detached threads
(a) Wrapping and needleweaving, detached buttonhole over a detached thread
(b) Detached buttonhole and buttonhole, all freely worked, not through the fabric
(c) Detached buttonhole worked over threads
(d) Zigzag chain over detached threads, wrapped threads and cretan over detached threads
(e) Buttonhole over detached threads
(f) Up and down buttonhole over detached threads
(g) Weaving over detached threads
(h) Wrapped detached threads, buttonhole over threads. Zigzag chain over threads, buttonhole over threads, all of which are detached
(i) Open chain over detached threads
(j) Buttonhole over detached threads

The background is charcoal linen with stitches in black, white, gold and raw sienna, in a variety of yarns including perle cotton numbers 3, 5 and 8, soft cotton and some wool

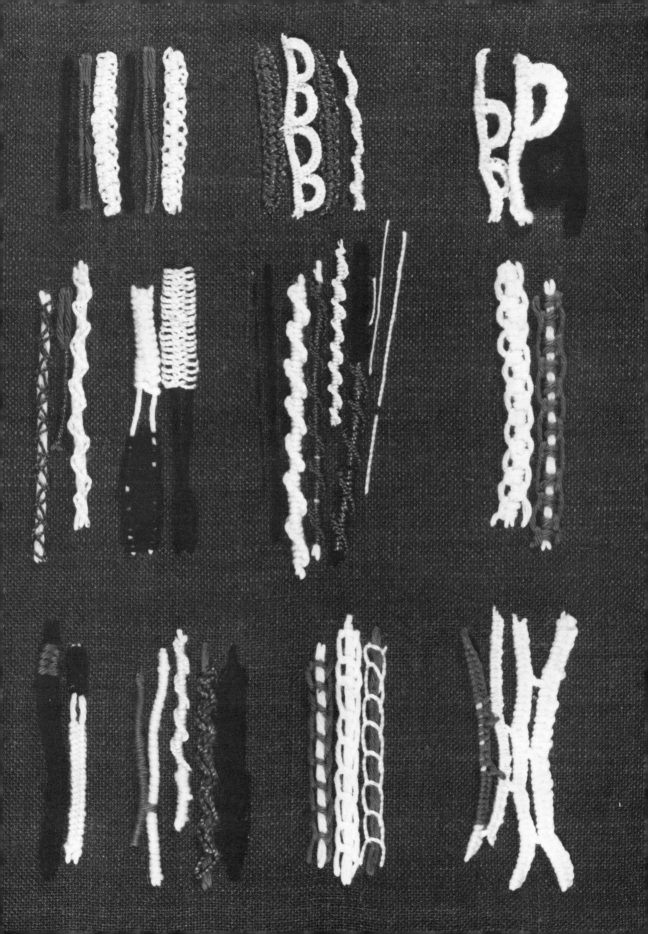

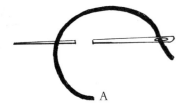

Bonnet stitch

So called as it was found on a bonnet in a 1923 copy of *Embroidery* Number 9.

Start at point A on the lower of two parallel lines. Pick up a small piece of fabric on the top line exactly opposite point A. Keep the thread under the needle. Take the thread under the loop and make a buttonhole stitch through the fabric and the base of the loop, bringing it out on the lower parallel line, ready for the next stitch.

Bonnet stitch *opposite*
The stitch is on scarlet cotton in white, variegated cream to ginger thread, dark and light brown and fawn, in perle cotton numbers 3, 5 and 8, weaving rayon, soft cotton, stranded cotton and fine coton-a-broder

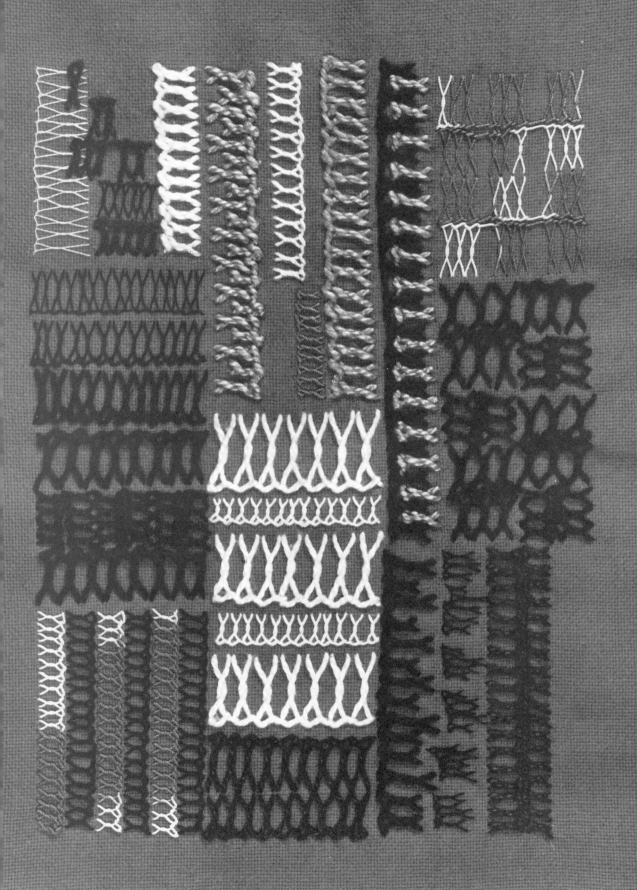

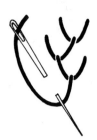

Feather stitch

Fly stitch

Feather stitch
A loop stitch with the structure of buttonhole. It has a number of varieties. Work from the top, vertically downwards

Feather stitch *opposite*
A variety of threads is used for this sampler. Perle cotton number 3, rayon, 1 strand of stranded cotton, sewing cotton, crochet cotton, raffine, nylon, slub cotton, soft nylon thread
The stitches are in white and cream on a blue fabric

Fly stitch *overleaf*
Fly stitch is a loop stitch with many variations.
It is worked from left to right, may be in rows or detached, overlapped or twisted.
On a pale grey background the stitches are in blacks and browns in sewing cotton, fine, fancy weaving yarns, tapestry wool, soft cotton and stranded cotton.

Fly stitch *page 61*
On an orange background, the stitches are in black yarns, including fine wool and coton-a-broder number 16, sewing cotton and fine weaving yarn, perle cotton number 8, soft cotton and a medium-weight wool.

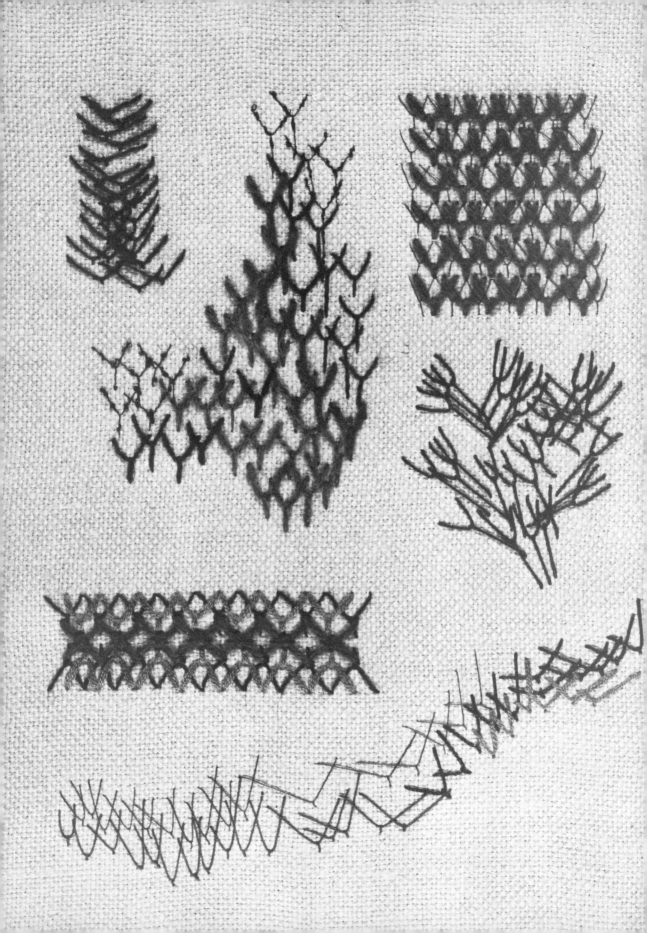

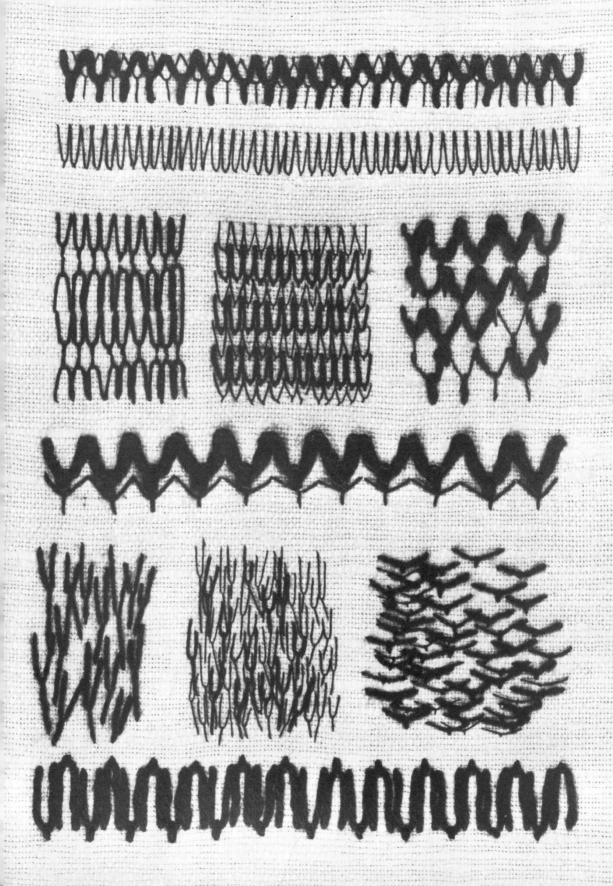

Twisted fly stitch

Work as for ordinary fly stitch but twist the thread over the needle at the base. To overlap, bring the needle up through to the middle of each stitch.

Fly with twisted chain

Fly stitch variations *opposite*

1 (a) Knotted fly – fine coton-a-broder two buttonhole at base
  (b) Twisted fly in number 5 perle cotton
  (c) Double row of fly with buttonhole number 3 perle
  (d) Twisted, crossed fly stitch. Number 8 perle
2   Fly with buttonhole. Number 5 perle cotton
3 (a) Fly with knots, perle number 8
  (b) Twisted fly, numbers 3 and 5 perle cotton
  (c) Fly stitch with buttonhole, number 5 perle cotton
  (d) Fly – slub threads
  (e) Crossed and twisted fly in spots
4 (a) Twisted fly, number 3 perle cotton
  (b) Perle cotton number 5
  (c) Sewing cotton
  (d) Slub thread
  (e) Perle cotton number 5
  (f) Number 12 coton-a-broder, detached fly with buttonhole
5 (a) Fly in 60 sewing cotton
  (b) Fly with buttonhole, perle cotton number 3
  (c) Fly, number 5 perle cotton
  (d) Twisted fly, number 5 perle cotton
6 (a) Twisted fly, number 5 perle cotton
  (b) Fly – perle number 5, with buttonhole
  (c) Fly with twisted chain, perle cotton number 5
  (d) Twisted fly, number 8 perle cotton
  (e) Fly with buttonhole, fine wool
  (f) Fly using two threads of different colours
Variegated colours from cream to light brown

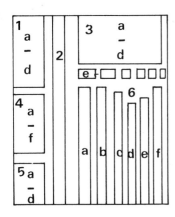

62

Sheaf stitch

Consists of groups of three or four straight stitches tied down with a horizontal one, in the middle. Freely interpreted the tying down stitch may be placed where wished as long as the group is tied

Sheaf filling stitch   *opposite*

Using a variety of yarns, from thick slubs, perle cotton number 5, coton-a-broder number 16, 1 strand of stranded cotton, and nylon weaving yarn, in black and white stitches on an orange background

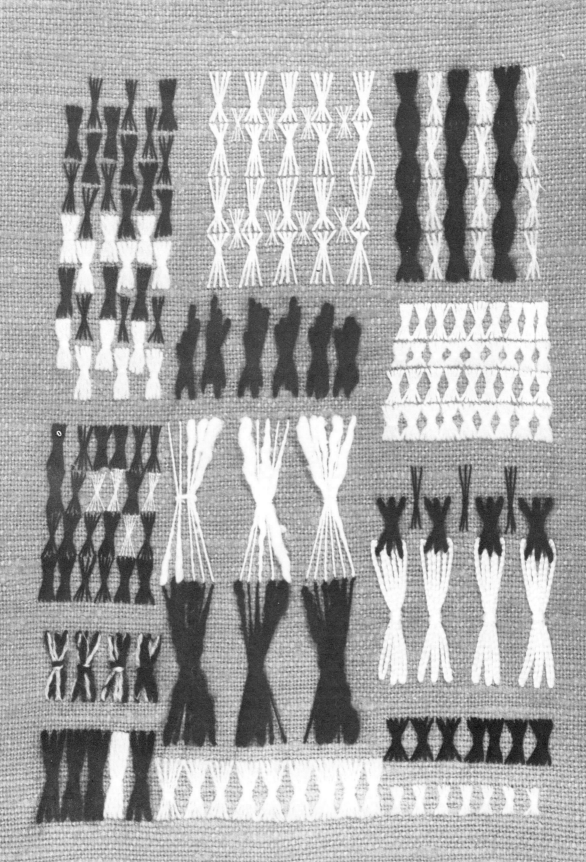

Sheaf stitch *opposite*
On a bright green background, the stitches are worked in white, cream and natural colours

Herringbone
Herringbone is extremely versatile. It may be worked openly and evenly in horizontal rows, closed to give two rows of back stitch on the wrong side of the work. It is used in shadow embroidery as double back stitch and is a basis of interlaced and tied stitches. It may be worked freely as detached stitches

Herringbone and closed herringbone   *opposite*
Wool, coton-a-broder number 16, perle cotton number 1, fine weaving yarn, fine wool, slub cotton, 1 strand of stranded cotton, raffine, rayon and other yarns give interesting textures. The stitches are in white on a dark greyish brown fabric

Herringbone and variations   *overleaf*
The herringbone stitches worked over one another to make heavy borders, must be very carefully spaced. The two top examples become vertically deeper, the one below becomes horizontally widened. They give an appearance of three dimensions and are interesting if worked in variegated colours of thread. The background is pale grey with stitches in white and cream in perle cotton number 5, soft cotton, 1 strand of stranded cotton, crochet cottons and synthetic yarns

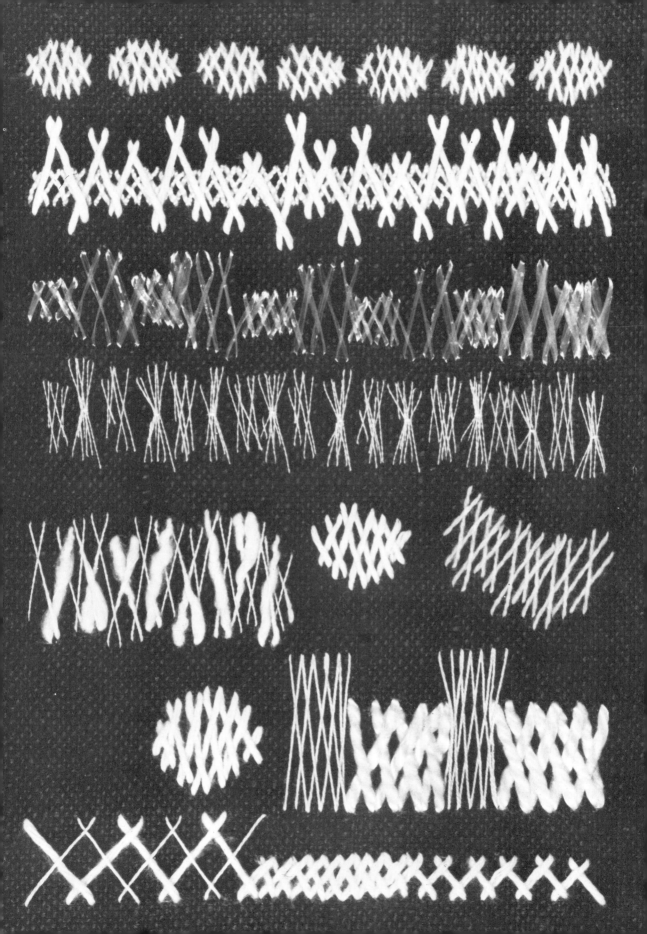

German interlacing or Maltese stitch and Interlaced herringbone

Make sure that the basic herringbone is correctly worked, before threading.

For interlaced herringbone, the needle is taken under the thread instead of over it.

Foundation for interlaced square

German interlacing

Interlaced herringbone *overleaf*
In white stitches on a turquoise background
(a) A selection of threads, fine crochet cotton, rayon, sewing cotton and thicker crochet cotton to give a variety of interlaced herringbone
(b) Interlacing and herringbone in two weights of wool
(c) Herringbone in fine crochet cotton, interlaced with thick wool
(d) Herringbone in fine wool with number 1 perle cotton for the interlacing
(e) Herringbone in fine crochet cotton interlaced with wool
(f) Herringbone in sewing cotton, with interlacing in fine crochet cotton

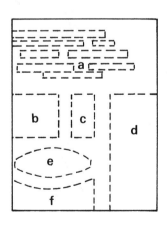

Interlaced square *page 73*
Perle cotton numbers 5 and 8, soft cotton, fine rayon, soft wool, coton-a-broder number 16
Sometimes the basic herringbone and the threading are of similar yarns, sometimes the herringbone is finer
The free adaptation is in various threads. The stitches are in white on a black background

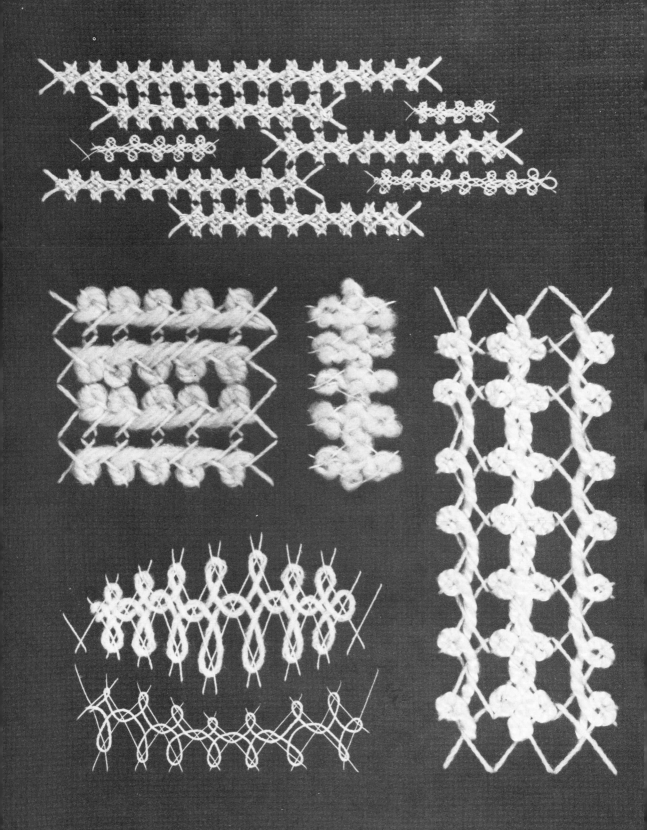

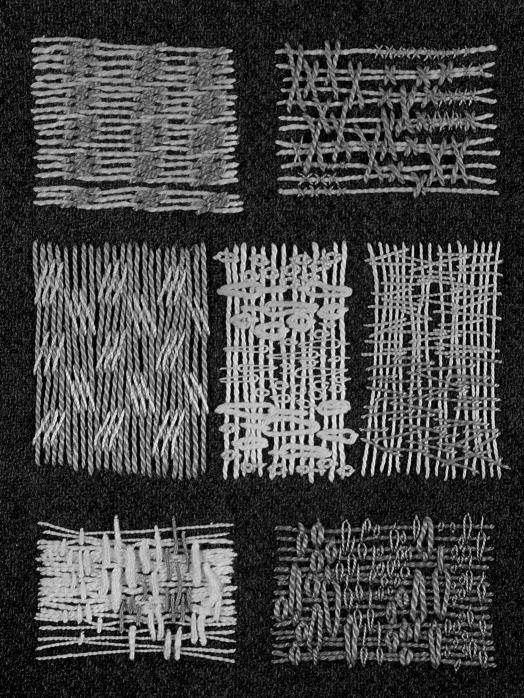

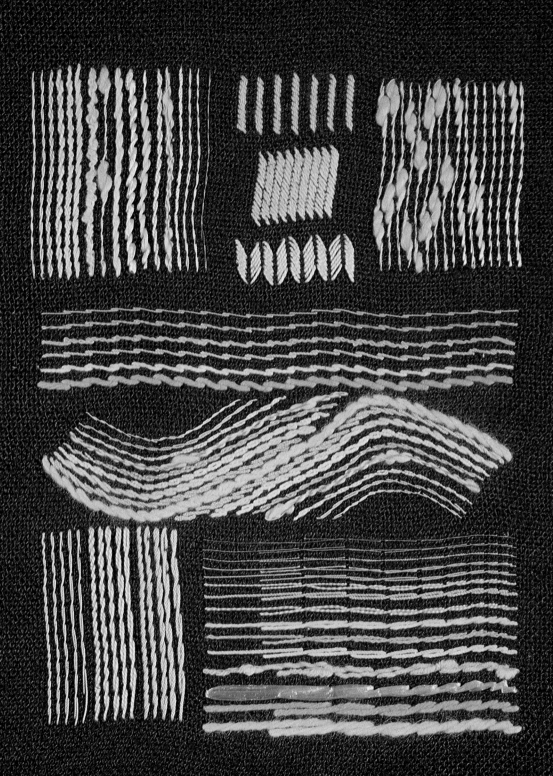

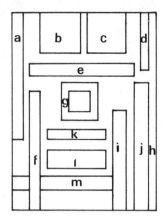

Herringbone and variations   *opposite*

(a) Herringbone with chain on the downward bar, perle cotton number 3
(b) Herringbone worked one way with the downward bar twisted. The alternate rows are worked the opposite way of the fabric, all in soft nylon
(c) Cut herringbone pile in wool
(d) Herringbone with twisted chain worked by turning fabric round
(e) Pile herringbone in wool, one row of overlapping herringbone
(f) Closed herringbone with a twist over the downward bar, worked from the bottom upwards in the illustration. Perle cotton number 3
(g) Closed, twisted herringbone in a square, perle cotton number 8
(h) Twisted herringbone with uneven spacing
(i) As (e) but with two channels and two rows of overlapping herringbone in nylon
(j) Open twisted herringbone in weaving yarn
(k) Herringbone with twisted chain
(l) Half herringbone, half cretan
(m) Herringbone with twisted chain and chain stitch, in weaving cotton

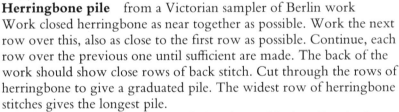

similar
yarns
weaving
cotton

The background is in charcoal coloured fabric with white stitches

Herringbone pile   from a Victorian sampler of Berlin work

Work closed herringbone as near together as possible. Work the next row over this, also as close to the first row as possible. Continue, each row over the previous one until sufficient are made. The back of the work should show close rows of back stitch. Cut through the rows of herringbone to give a graduated pile. The widest row of herringbone stitches gives the longest pile.

For a high pile in the middle of a band, two blocks of herringbone stitches must be worked, until sufficient rows are made to meet one another. Cut through both blocks and the highest pile will be in the middle, with half bands on each side. If these are not required they may be cut out

For a high domed square, on the straight, draw the square and extend on its points to give a square on the cross, surrounding the straight square. Continue going round, each row becoming shorter but gradually filling the triangles of the outer square and those within the first square, until there is no space and probably only one wide herringbone stitch. Cut through all the rows and the high pile will be in the middle of the square. The four triangles outside may be left, may become parts of new squares or may be removed

Each row of herringbone may be in a different colour and texture of thread, if wished

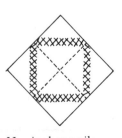

Herringbone pile

74

Knotted herringbone   heavy stiff thread

1   Work herringbone from the top downwards but with the needle pointing upwards. (Normally herringbone is worked from left to right.)

2 and 3   Work a twisted chain on each bar – the top or bottom only can be worked, if wished, not through the fabric.

4   If closed herringbone is worked, a thick band results. Spacing is important here.

5 and 6   To add to the weight, thread through under the herringbone bar and the tail of the twisted chain, working a chain round each twisted chain as stitch proceeds. Work through the fabric to hold this chain stitch

Invented stitch

Variation on herringbone, closed and looped.
The first stitch may be worked vertically downwards, or diagonally.
The threading is slightly different, the result different

Invented stitch
Herringbone with twisted
chain surrounded with chain

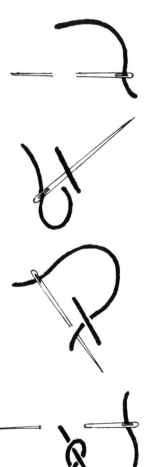

Invented stitch
Herringbone with
twisted chain

Closed herringbone
with loop

Herringbone variation

Gives a close twisted stitch. Work one diagonal stitch, thread from right to left, then work a diagonal stitch with a threading over this. The diagrams explain the method clearly.

This stitch is a variation that looks like herringbone. It consists of threading which should be pulled tightly after each process to make knots. The result has the appearance of a tied herringbone

Keep within 2 parallel lines

Start with a diagonal stitch worked from left to right, bottom to top. Thread back into the stitch and then into the loop as in the diagram. Take a stitch on the base line to the right and thread back in to the diagonal one. Thread into the loop made; continue, pulling the loops tightly after threading

a

b

Invented stitch

Giving an effect of closed herringbone with a twist in the centre, worked between two parallel lines. The diagram shows the procedure.

(a) Work from right to left, making a diagonal line downwards. Bring the needle out below and opposite the thread above

(b) Thread under the diagonal stitch, not through the fabric, bringing the needle over the stitch and under the loop made, not through the fabric (c)

(d) Take the needle horizontally through the upper line, equidistant amounts of fabric being taken up on either side of the first stitch. Proceed to the next diagonal stitch. A thick yarn gives good results

c

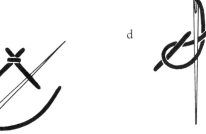

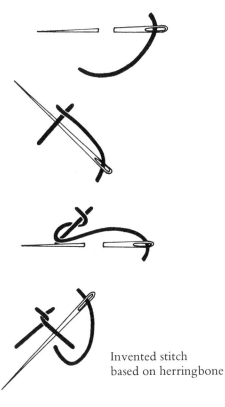

Invented stitch
based on herringbone

d

Tied herringbone

Chevron   *opposite*
In coffee coloured linen with white stitching in a variety of yarns, perle cotton number 5 and 8, slub cotton, soft cotton, sewing cotton, coton-a-broder number 16, 1 strand of stranded cotton and fine nylon.

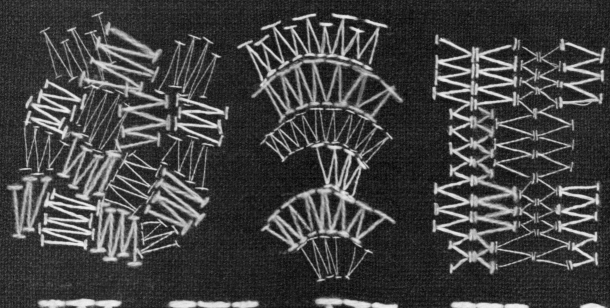

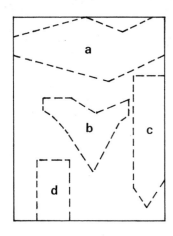

Chevron *opposite*

Dark brown fabric with white stitches in

(a) Number 16 coton-a-broder, fine cotton, sewing cotton, 1 strand of stranded cotton
(b) Coton-a-broder number 16, 1 strand of stranded cotton
(c) 1 strand of stranded cotton, number 16 coton-a-broder, sewing cotton
(d) Wool worked over 2 strands of stranded cotton

Cretan basically a loop stitch
Cretan is very versatile and can be altered considerably by taking up smaller or larger amounts of fabric in the needle, by its spacing and the angle at which the needle enters the fabric. The cross–over when changed can be made a design feature of the stitch. It may be worked vertically with the needle vertical, or with it horizontal or slightly diagonal as in stitching leaf shapes. It is effective in a circle or worked freely and diagonally. Twisted chain may be worked on the bars

Cretan and variations *opposite*
Regular, irregular, overlapping. The stitches are in white and cream, the background dark brown. Threads used are sewing cotton, 1 and 2 strands of stranded cotton, soft cotton, slub cotton and perle cotton number 8

Cretan and variations *overleaf*
Freely worked on a dark brown ground with stitches in white and cream. 1 strand of stranded cotton with china beads, also white; stranded cotton from 1 to 6 threads, fancy weaving yarns and sewing cottons are used for the sampler which shows an invented cretan stitch in the second row down

Cretan *page 85*
A dull green background is worked in white and cream yarns in weaving yarns, perle cotton numbers 3, 5 and 8 and 1 strand of stranded cotton

Cretan and variations

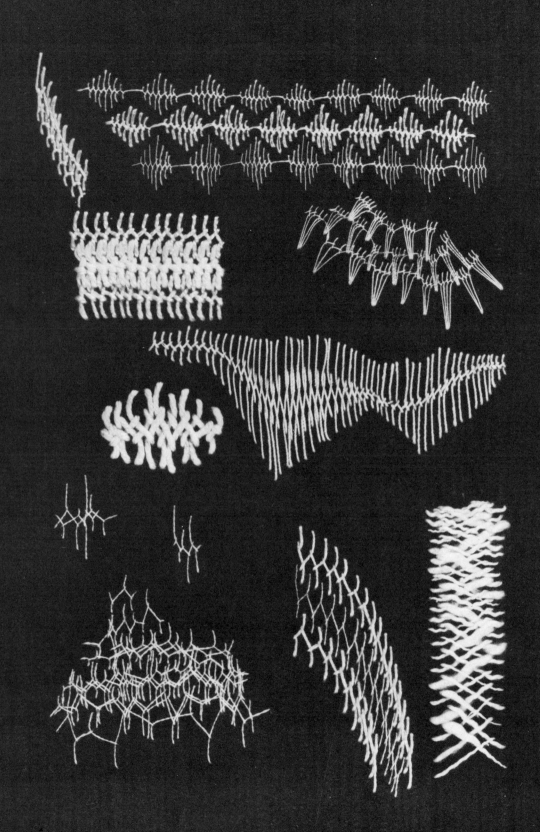

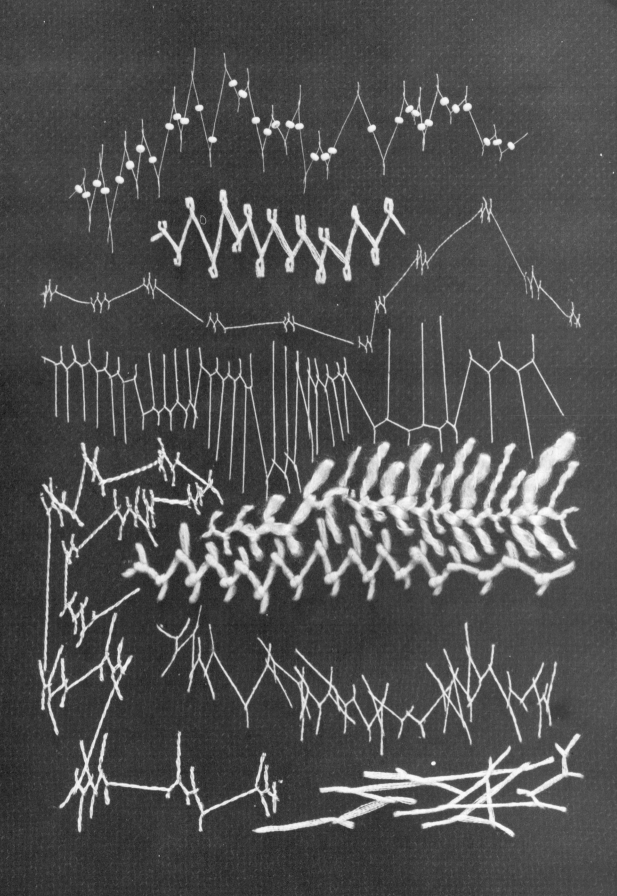

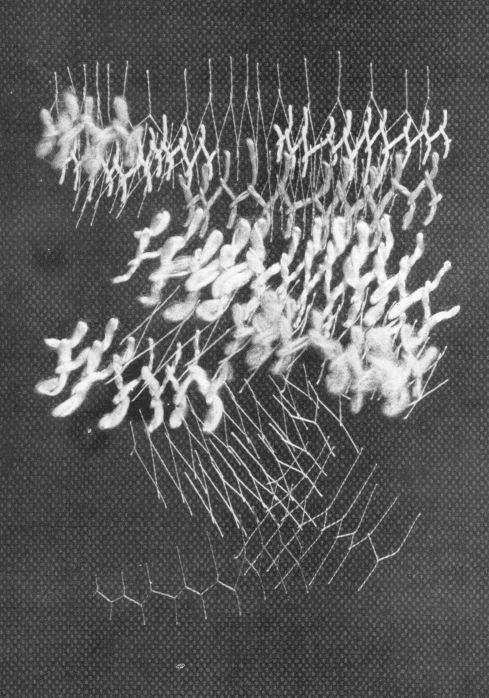

Wave stitch
Start with a row of spaced straight stitches. Thread the following row, taking up a small piece of fabric at the base of each stitch. The ensuing row is threaded into the previous one. By making irregular lengths of stitch very interesting surface textures result

Wave stitch *opposite*
Worked regularly but in the centre block the basic vertical stitches are unevenly aligned to give a freer result. This stitch is very versatile, giving close or open textures and with the length of stitch and the choice of yarns, an appearance of depth. Slub cotton, wool, soft cotton, stranded cotton, coton-a-broder number 16 and perle cotton numbers 3, 5 and 8 are used for the stitches which are in variegated cream to fawn thread, white and cream, on dull green fabric

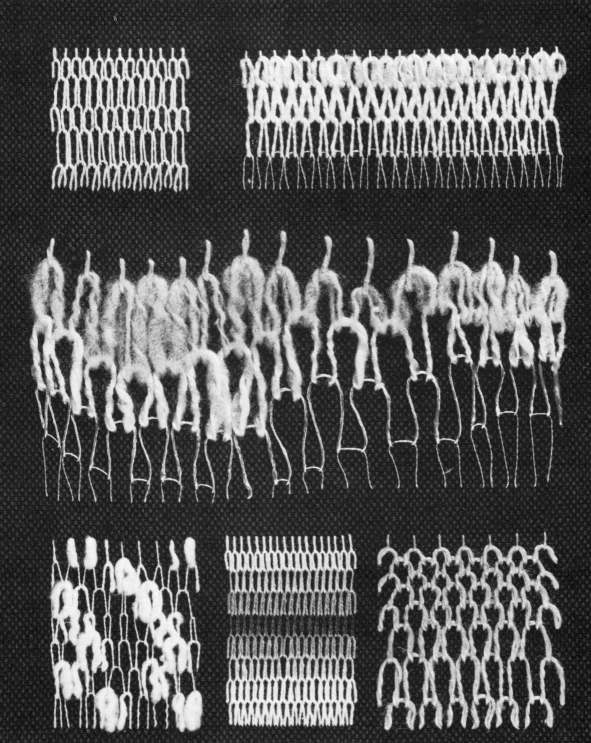

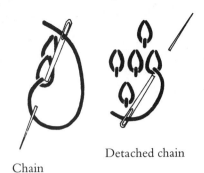

Detached chain

Chain

Chain stitch
(a) A loop stitch with many variations. It may be used as a line, as a solid filling, detached, as a band and if worked in different directions gives good tonal changes
Detached chain, sometimes called lazy daisy

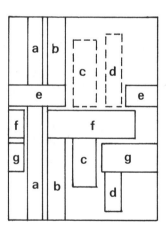

Chain stitch *opposite*
(a) Sewing cotton with split raffine
(b) Perle cotton number 5
(c) Twisted rayon, with crochet rayon and perle cotton number 5
(d) Sewing thread
(e) Coton-a-broder with split raffine
(f) Slub weaving yarn
(g) Fine wool
Cream and white stitches are worked on a brown ground

Detached chain *overleaf*
In soft cotton
Perle cotton number 8, sewing cotton
Slub cotton
Fine wool
Raffine and fine wool
1 strand of stranded cotton
Coton-a-broder number 16
Twisted rayon and fine wool
1 strand of stranded cotton and fine wool
Twisted weaving yarn and rayon
In white and cream stitches on a charcoal background

Detached chain *page 91*
Using a variety of yarns. Perle numbers 5 and 8, wool, sewing cotton, rayon, soft cotton, nylon, split raffine, fancy weaving yarn, coton-a-broder number 12
In white stitches on a grey blue fabric

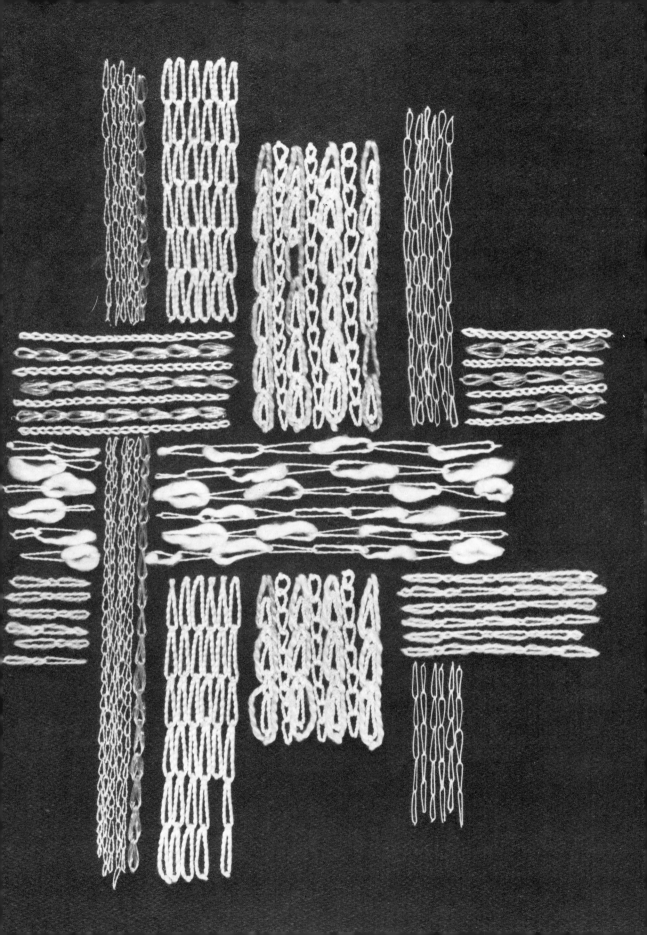

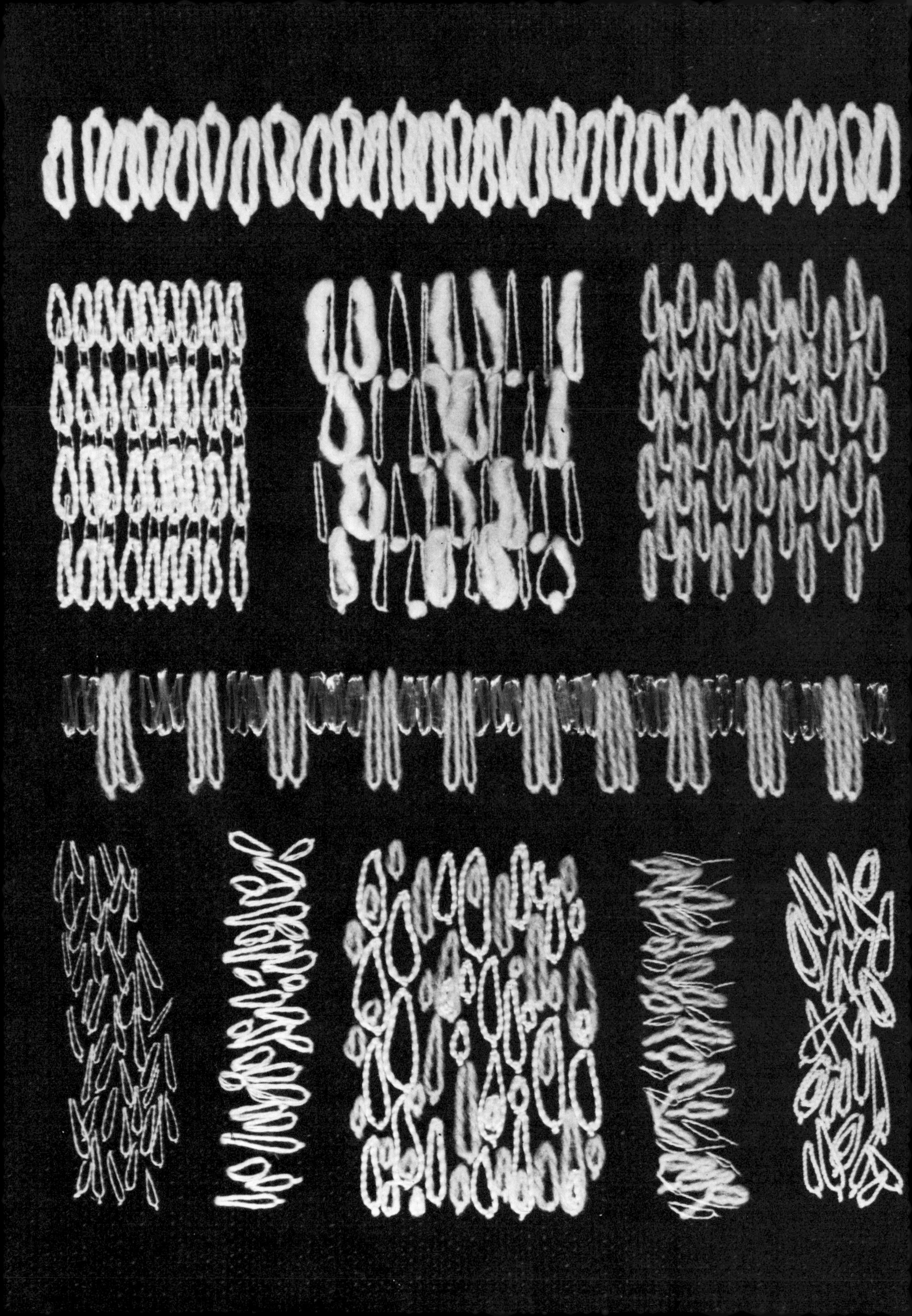

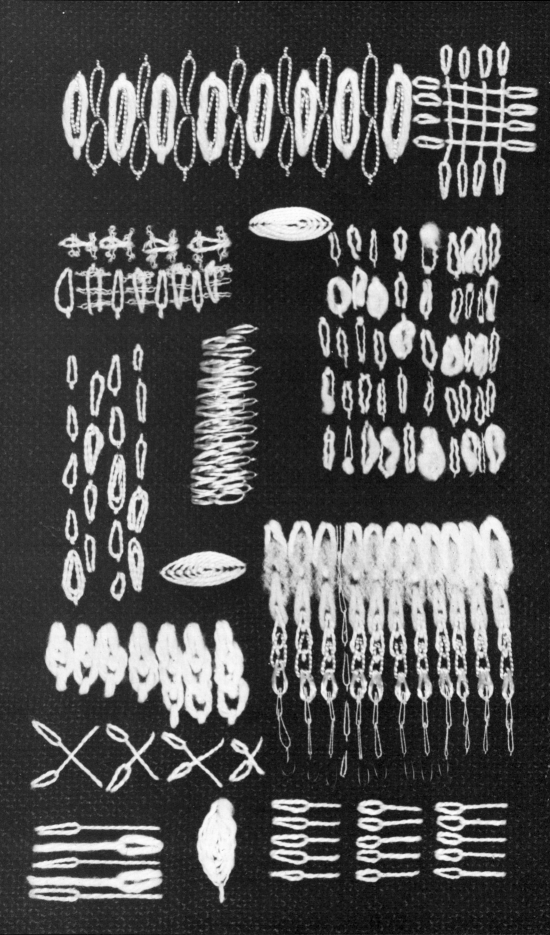

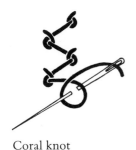

Coral knot

Coral knot and zigzag chain

Coral knot is a variation of twisted chain, with more space between each stitch. The angle at which the needle enters the fabric also gives a different appearance to the stitch

Zigzag chain – consists of twisted chain worked as a band rather than a line

Zigzag chain and variations   *opposite*

Fine to coarse threads, wool, cotton, nylon, coton-a-broder number 12, rayon, 1 strand of stranded cotton and slub cotton are used for the stitches in white on a black background fabric

Twisted chain

Twisted chain (straight)   Variations of zigzag coral   *overleaf*

Various threads including soft cotton, weaving yarns, perle cottons number 5 and 8, are used for the stitches which are in brown and black yarns on a grey background

Twisted chain or coral stitch   *opposite*

Worked soft cotton, wool, perle cotton numbers 5 and 8, wool, crochet cotton, coton-a-broder number 16. Black and several shades of brown yarn are worked on a pale grey background

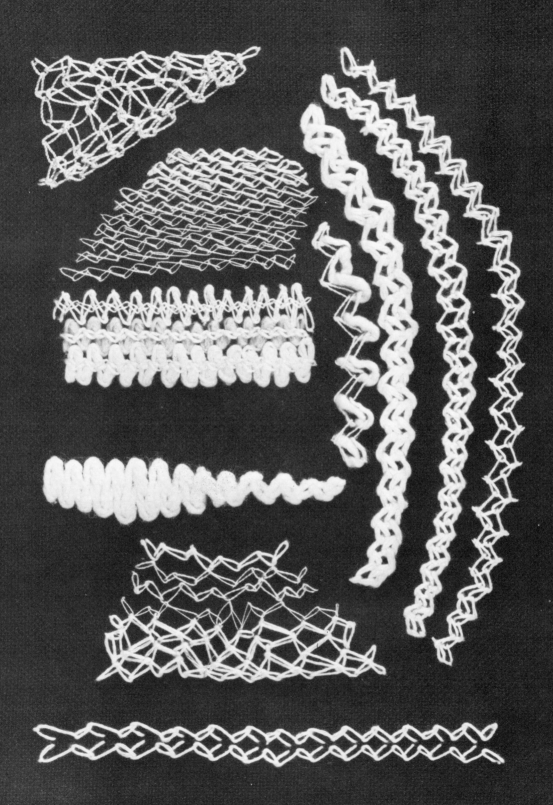

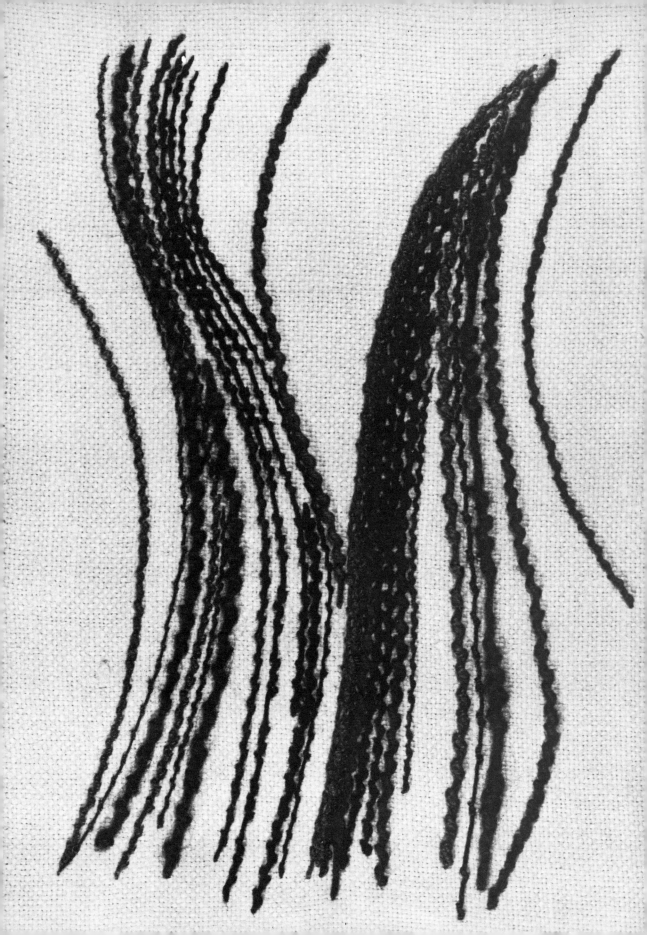

Zigzag coral and variations   *page 95*
With formal and free interpretations in weaving yarns, perle cottons
numbers 5 and 8, and sewing cotton
The stitches are in brown, black and cream on a pale grey fabric

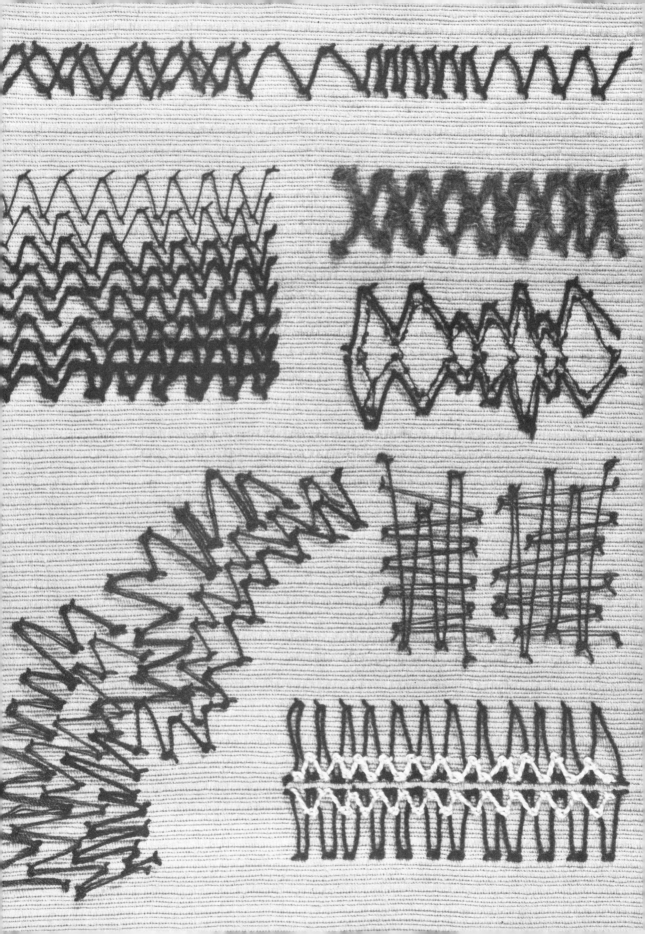

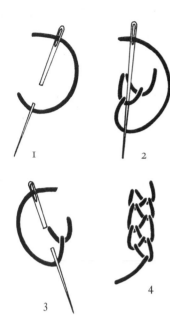

1   2

3   4

Double chain *opposite*
A variety of threads – slub cotton, soft cotton, sewing cotton, 2 strands of stranded cotton, lurex, perle cotton number 5, fine weaving cotton. The stitches are in black on a pale grey fabric

Cable chain

Cable chain *left*
The usual method is to twist the thread over the needle

Easy cable chain *below left*
Take a vertical running stitch and come out below, as for broad chain. Thread from right to left and again through loop. Insert needle below to make another running stitch and down to start again
Variation – knot the last loop before making the next running stitch

Easy cable chain

Overleaf
Double chain and variations (circle)
Stranded cotton, fine wool, perle cotton numbers 3, 5 and 8, soft cotton give depth, with black stitches worked on pale grey fabric

Cable chain variation *page 101*
This is an easy method of working a stitch which gives an appearance of cable chain. In this way a great divergence of lengths of stitch are possible. Thick wool, fancy weaving yarns, rayon and fine crochet cotton are used for the white stitches on a maroon background

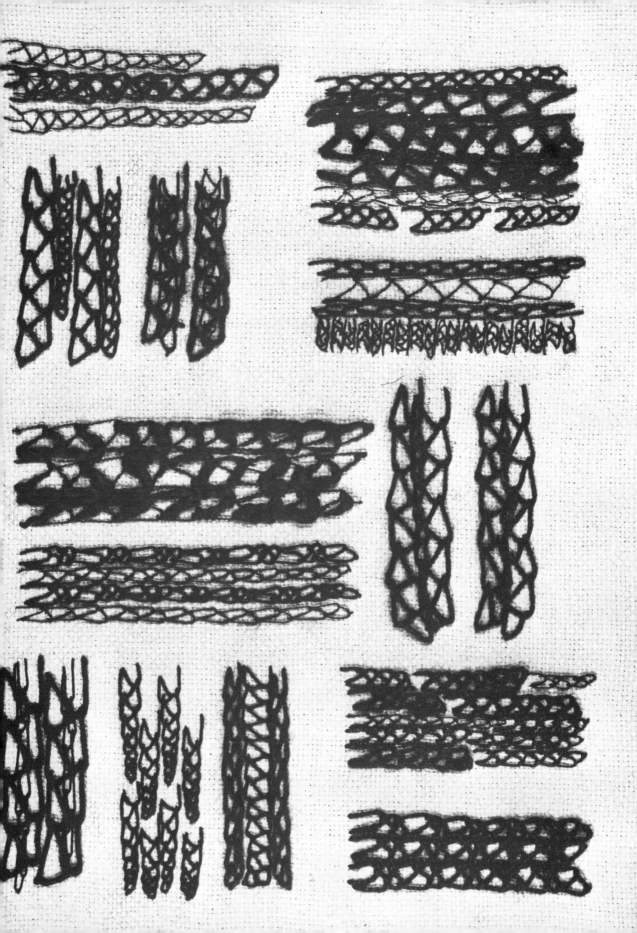

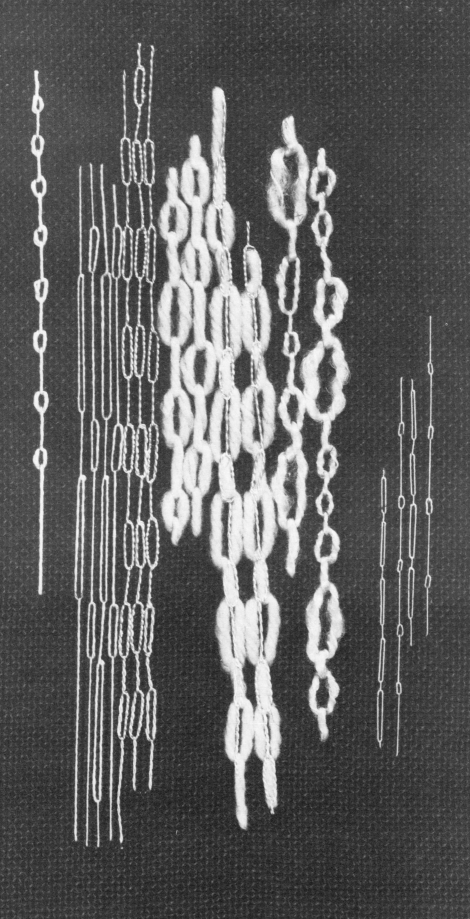

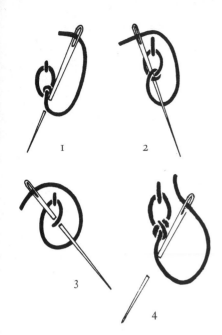

Knotted cable chain variation *opposite*

Much elongated, in a variety of threads, sewing cotton, 1 strand of stranded cotton, fine wool, perle cotton numbers 5 and 8, soft cotton slub cotton, weaving threads. The stitches are in variegated cream to fawn, cream thread and white on a charcoal background

Stitch based on open chain medium to heavier weight yarns give the best results. Firm ones are better than soft ones

1   Work a vertical twisted chain.
2   Take needle horizontally to right (6 mm–12 mm/¼ in.–½ in. according to weight of thread). Make another vertical twisted chain, which may be level or below the first stitch. If right handed, the thread must here be twisted over the needle; if left handed the stitch on the left side must have the thread twisted over the needle
3   Return to (1), taking the needle through the first stitch and down vertically again, then across to the right side
4   Each time two bars are made horizontally, they may be tied together with twisted chain
   Alternately, this occurs from the left and the right, when the thread must be twisted over the needle
   The bars may be left untied as required

See sampler page 107 group (c)

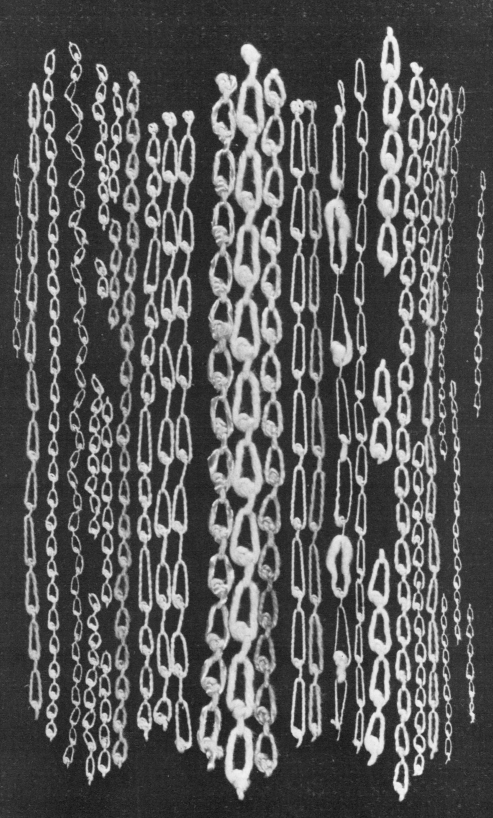

Rosette chain
The structure of this stitch is basically twisted chain threaded
Use a stiff thread for good results.

Rosette chain   *opposite*
Fine and coarse threads
Perle cottons numbers 5 and 8, wool, soft cotton, crochet cotton,
coton-a-broder number 16
The stitches are in variegated thread, white to pale coffee colour and
white on a charcoal background

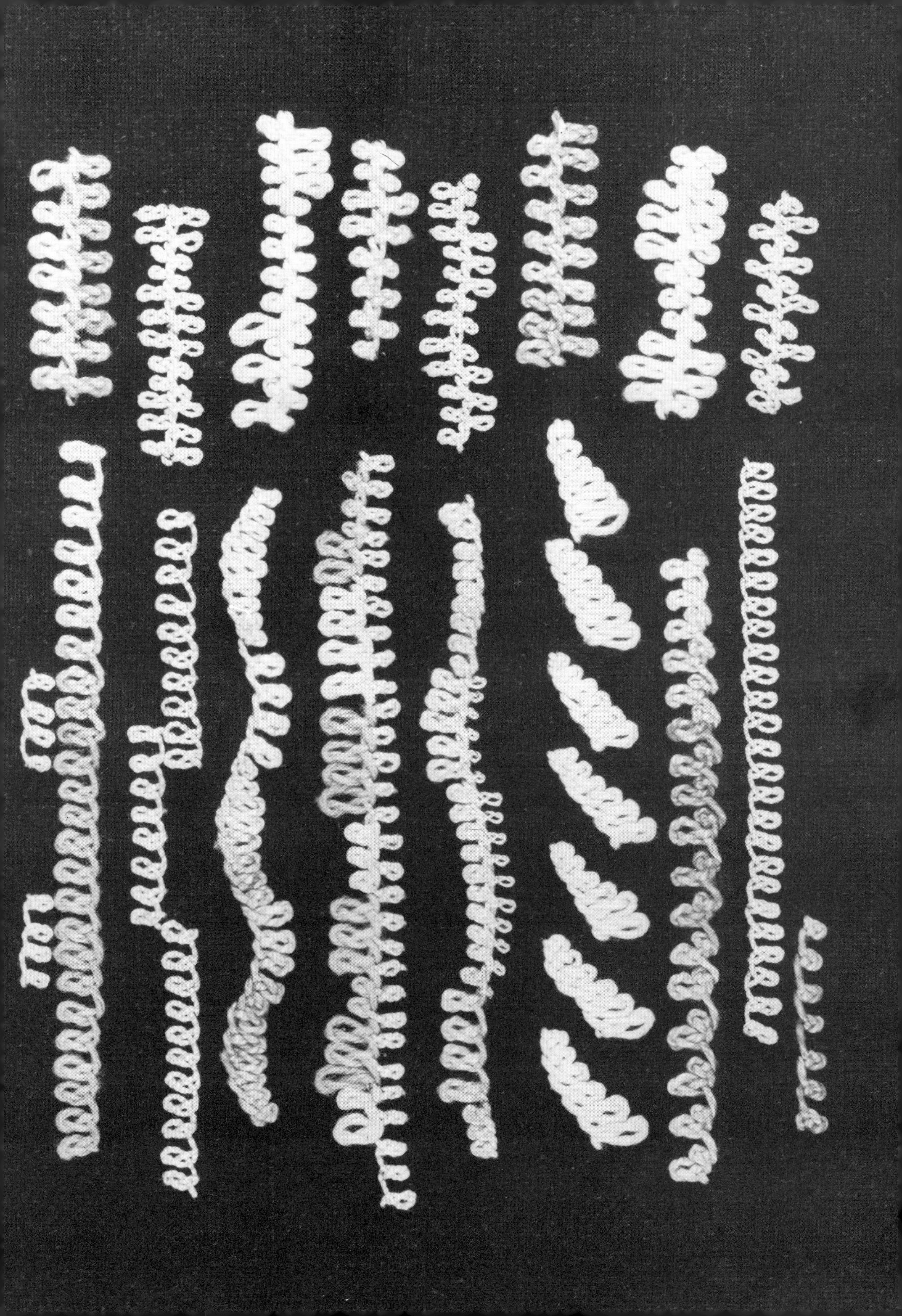

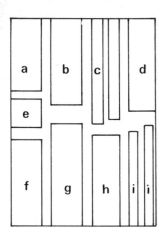

Variations on twisted chain, link chain and others *opposite*
Group (a) Variation on twisted chain
Group (b) Link chain worked the easy way
Group (c) Variation on open chain using twisted chain
Group (d) Variations on twisted chain, worked from top to bottom and also reversed
Group (e) (Small block) zigzag chain and variation
Group (f) Chain with twisted chain
Group (g) Double chain with buttonhole and variations
Group (h) Easy cable chain knotted
Group (i) An invented stitch that looks similar to tied herringbone
A number of different yarns are used for these stitches, including perle cottons numbers 5 and 8, tied and dyed crochet cotton, soft cotton

(g)

Double chain
Variation   double chain with buttonhole
Two, three or more buttonhole stitches may be worked on the loops of double chain, as required. More stitches can be devised from double chain with buttonhole. The needle down and out below, ready for the next threading.

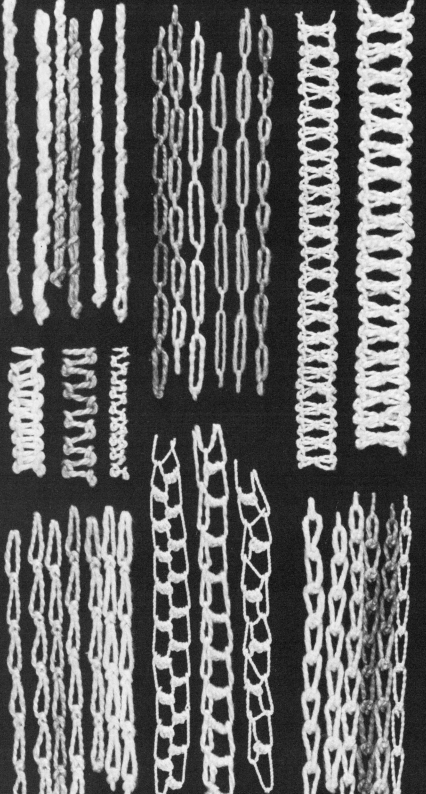

Open chain

Sometimes called square chain. A versatile stitch, requiring good tension in working.

Heavy chain

Work heavy chain but take up the centre of each one before the last stitch, instead of taking the needle through the previous but one stitch. This makes a good braid. Instead one side of the understitch can be taken up by the needle. This gives a different appearance

Heavy chain variation

Commence as for broad chain, but take the needle two loops back for threading, not one as in broad chain

Open chain

left block page 109

Heavy chain

right block page 109

Open or square chain and heavy chain with variations   *opposite*

Worked in white, mauve and honey coloured yarns on a greenish grey fabric.

> Open chain with varying scales and the position of the bars (top left)
> Heavy chain and variations (bottom right)

Soft cotton, perle cottons numbers 5 and 8, fine crochet cotton, coton-a-broder and a single strand of stranded cotton are used for the stitches

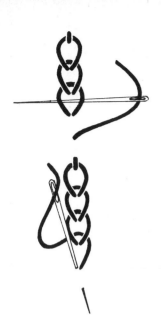

Broad chain
Start with a vertical straight stitch
Bring the needle out below and thread back from right to left through the stitch to make a loop. Continue

Solid fillings *opposite*
The directions in which the stitches are worked give strong tonal variations to the results
Open chain variations with chain stitch
Stem stitch
Satin stitch
Different types of yarn are used, stranded cotton, perle cotton numbers 3, 5 and 8, rayon, coton-a-broder number 12. The stitches are in white and cream on a green background

Wheatear
Wheatear may be continuous or detached, worked vertically downwards

Wheatear *overleaf*
Here an effect of diminishing tone and dimension is obtained by the weight of thread, changing from coarse to fine
Soft cotton, perle cottons numbers 5 and 8, fine wool, stranded cotton in 3, 2 and 1 strands to 6 strands and rayon are used
The stitches are white on a black background.

Wheatear *page 113*
Freely interpreted with variations
Coarse nylon thread, soft cotton, coton-a-broder, sewing thread and very fine weaving yarn are employed

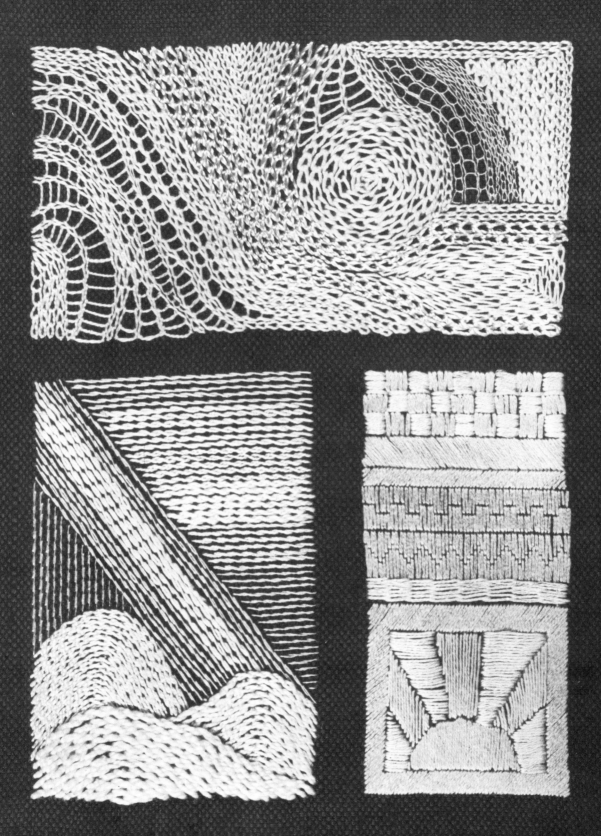

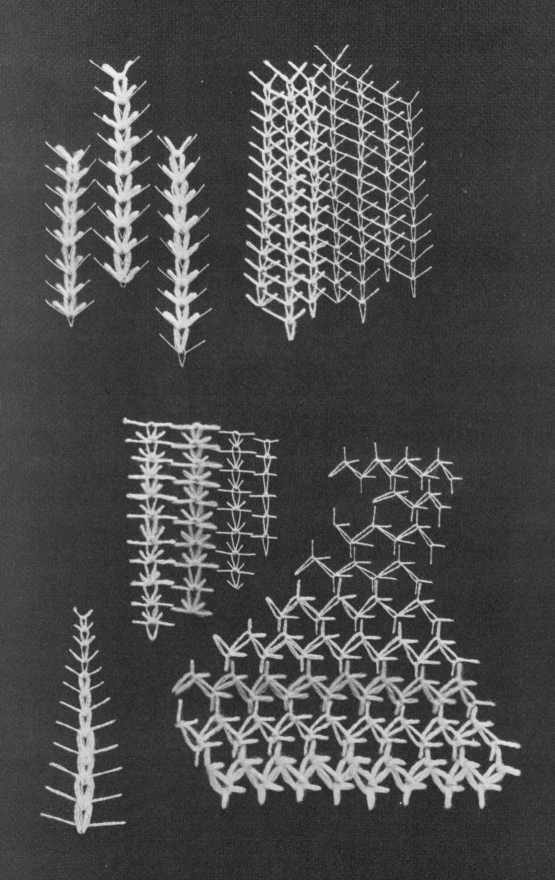

French knots

When the thread has been twisted once a or twice round the needle, insert it just to the side of the emerging thread.

Knots *opposite*

French knot, Chinese knots and threaded crosses, are worked in white in soft cotton, perle cotton numbers 3 and 5, 1 strand of stranded cotton and sewing cotton, on a tan background fabric

French knots are worked in a variety of threads including one strand of stranded cotton, perle numbers 5 and 8 and soft cotton. Threaded crosses are worked in soft cotton

Threaded cross

Bullion knots with and without tails *overleaf*

The curved bands show the two kinds of bullion worked vertically and horizontally in various weights of thread

The top group of knots is in various weights of thread, sometimes looped

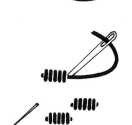

The lower group of knots is in various weights of thread with tails made by taking up a longer piece of fabric in the needle but wrapping only a third or half the distance or loops made by taking up small pieces of fabric but with longer twistings. Soft cotton, weaving yarns, medium weight wool in yellows, brown, ochre, creams, gold and white are worked on a green background

Bullion knots

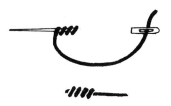

Bullion knots *page 117*

Stars in wool, rayon, coton-a-broder number 6

The rest of the sampler in fine crochet cotton, medium weight wool, and coarse and fine rayon

This selection of threads gives a good, raised texture. White stitches are worked on a reddish purple linen

Bullion knots with tails

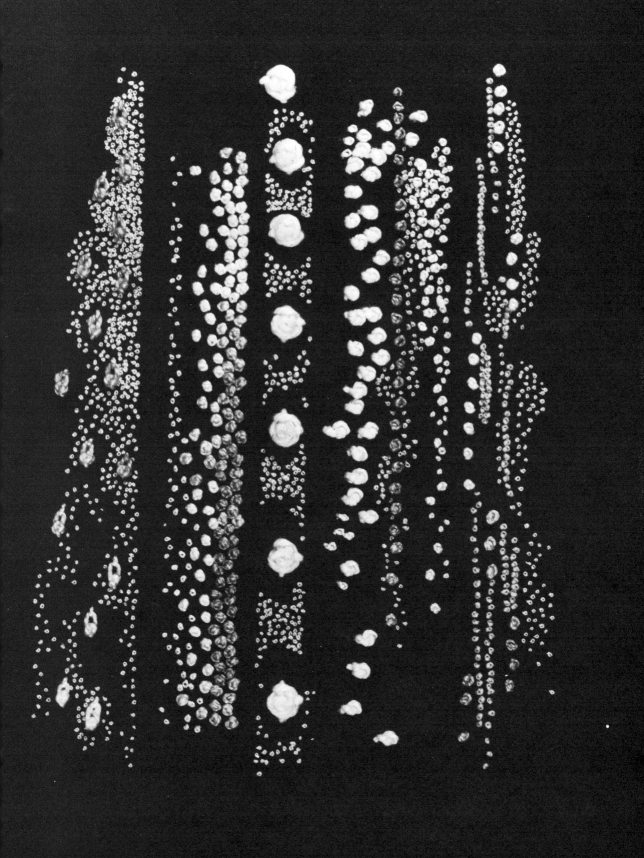

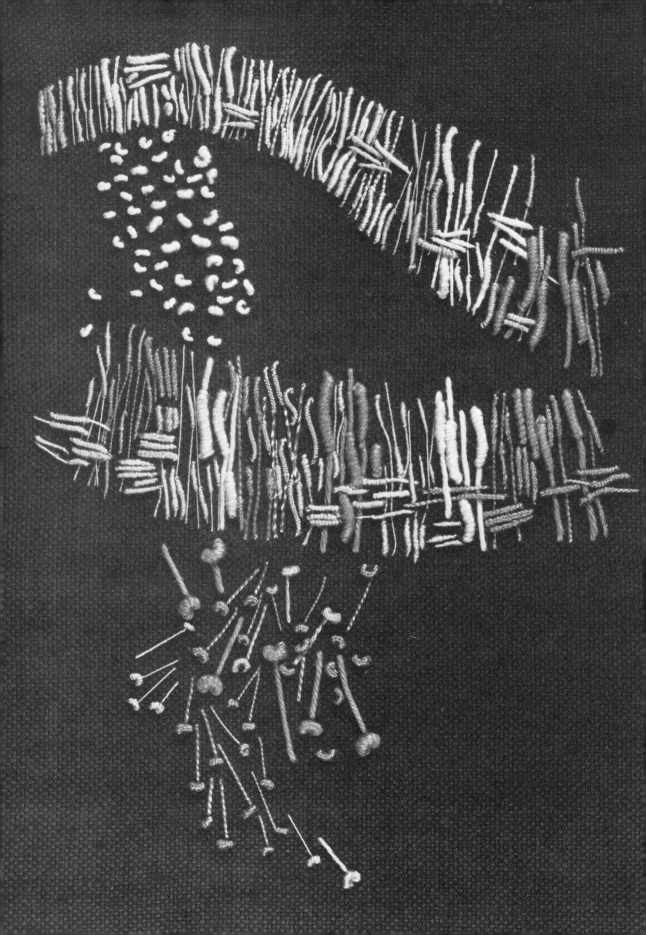

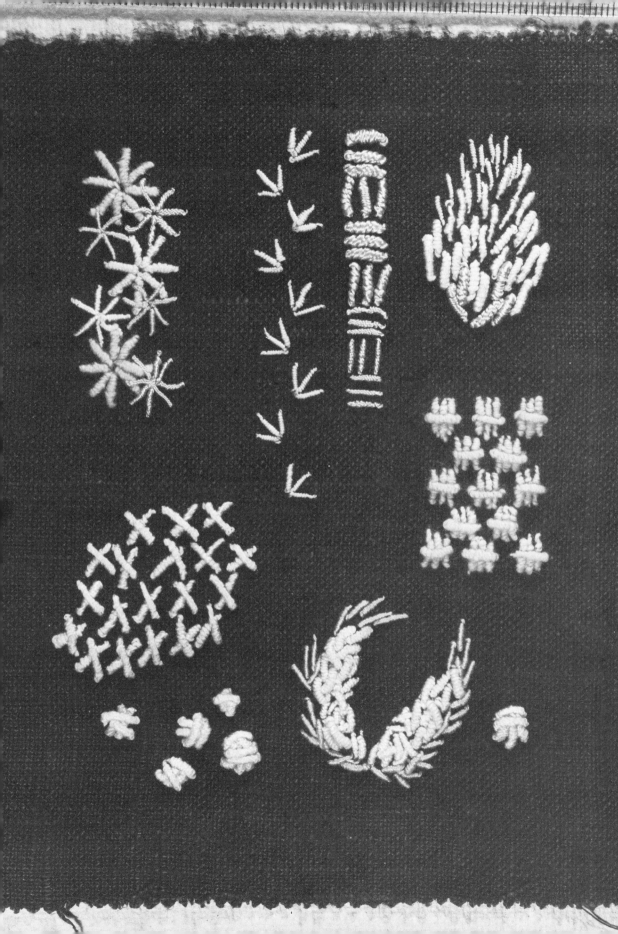

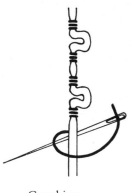

Couching

Roumanian couching

Couching

Couching is a method of tying down one thread or several threads with another. For lines or to fill areas. It may be varied considerably by the choice of textures and colours combined differently. Threads may be tied down with quite different stitches sometimes almost invisibly, sometimes half concealing them.

A thick thread pulled up in loops which are kept in place with groups of couching stitches

Roumanian couching is usually worked to fill an area, the tying down thread and the couched thread being one and the same so that each is indistinguishable

Couching *opposite*

From top

Soft wool couched with herringbone in fine thread
Heavy weaving yarn, couched with cretan in fine rayon
Heavy weaving yarn couched with herringbone in wool
carded fleece couched with chevron in 1 strand of stranded cotton
Heavy weaving wool couched with fly stitch
Wool couched with cretan stitch using from 1 to 3 threads of stranded cotton
Wool couched in zigzag chain in weaving yarn
Soft wools couched with chevron in 2 strands of cotton and in wool in herringbone
Wools couched in 2 strands of cotton with crossed, detached chain

The background is an orange fabric with a number of colours for the couched threads and stitches: magenta, brown, dark prune, cream, ochre, burnt sienna. The colours are arranged in different combinations so that they sometimes give the appearance of more colours than are used for the sample

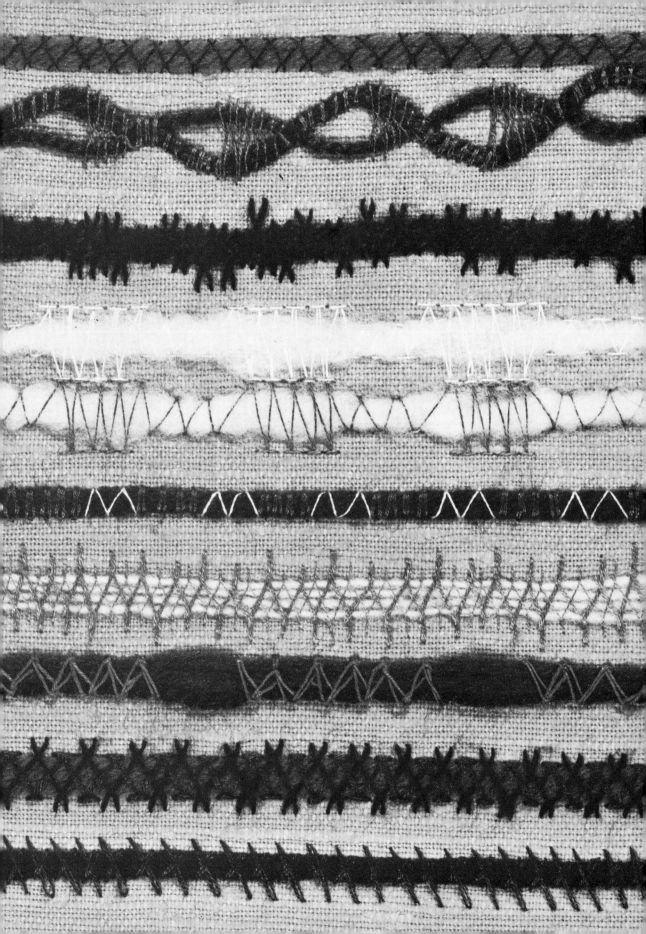

Couching *opposite*
The background is dark brown with stitches in light brown, gold,
yellow, greenish-yellow and pale pinks
> A variety of yarns is used including (from top)
> Medium weight wools couched in herringbone in a fancy
> weaving yarn
> Heavy weaving yarn couched with fly stitch in a fine weaving
> yarn
> Very fine rayon couched with a heavier rayon
> Plastic thread rather like straw couched in fine, twisted rayon
> rayon couched with finer rayon
> Chenille couched in buttonhole (upside-down) in rayon
> Weaving yarn couched with herringbone in rayon and coton-a-
> broder number 16
> Weaving yarn couched in 2 strands of stranded cotton
> Heavy weaving yarn couched with zigzag coral stitch
> Chenille couched with stranded cotton (2 strands)
> Raffine couched with feather stitch in fine weaving yarns
> Fine rayon weaving yarns couched with fly stitch in fine rayon

Roumanian stitch *page 123*
Heavy and fine weights of yarn, perle cotton number 5, coton-a-
broder, 1 strand of cotton, soft cotton, sewing cotton and wool give
strongly contrasting textures, in black stitching on a pale grey
background

Roumanian stitch *overleaf*
Heavy and fine threads, perle cotton number 5, soft cotton, weaving
yarns, fine and coarse wools, stranded cotton, all together create good
contrasts of texture. The background is pale grey with black and white
stitches

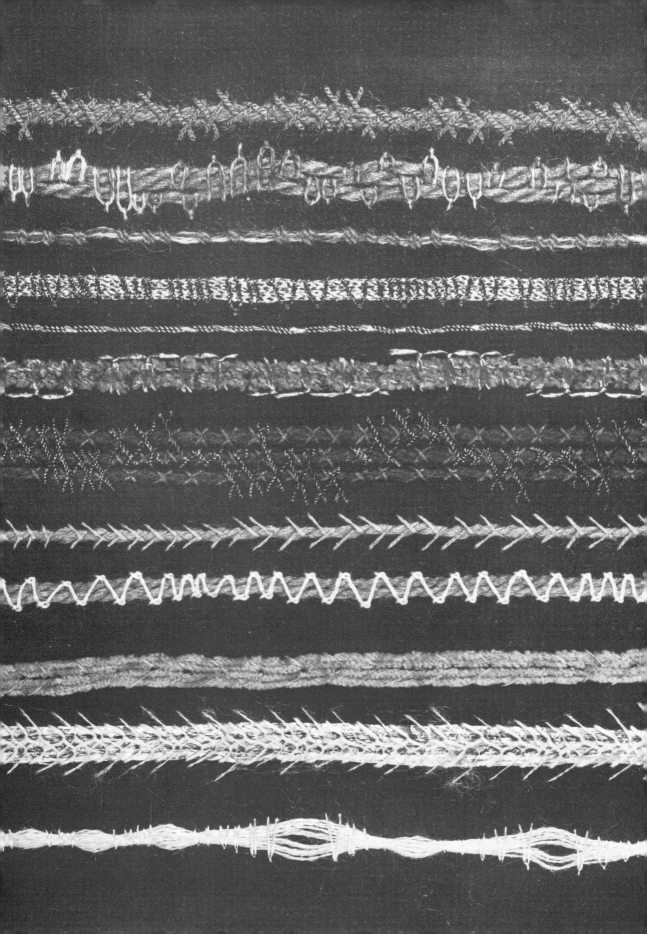

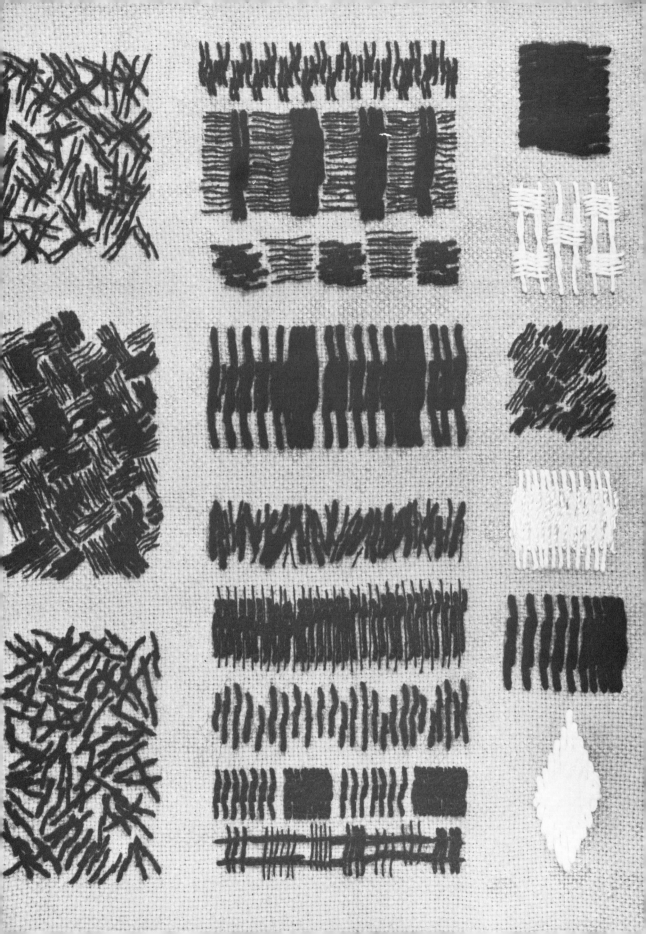

Thorn stitch *opposite*
One thread is used for the spine and the stitch which ties it down.
It is useful on curved lines and can be worked with regular crossing
threads or quite irregularly. It may consist of a separate thread for the
spine. The diagram shows one version of working it which is easy.
The other one is the usual method

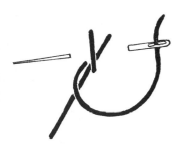

Thorn stitch
Easy method with
one thread

Thorn stitch
Usual method
with two threads

Thorn stitch *opposite*
Worked in white on a dark brown background. In soft wool, fancy
weaving yarns, poodle wool, crochet cotton and sewing cotton

Raised chain band

Raised chain band
Worked over bars, regularly spaced.
Irregular running stitches make the background for freely worked raised chain band which gives an attractive texture

Raised chain band *opposite*
A variety of threads is used, fine and coarse, slubs, rayon, fine wools, nylon, number 16 coton-a-broder, perle cotton number 8, for the free interpretation of the stitch which is worked in white and cream on a bright red background. Sometimes the basic structure of bars is finer than the raised chain, sometimes it is similar in weight of thread. A non-stretchy thread should be used for the bars to give a crisp result

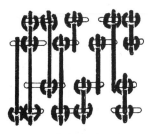

Raised chain band

Raised stem band

Raised stem band *overleaf*
A structure of bars is necessary, as for raised chain band. These may be evenly or unevenly spaced with stitches worked at right angles to them. Slub cotton, weaving yarns, perle cotton numbers 3, 5 and 8 and soft cotton are worked over the bars as well as for the bars, to give lively textural bands. Variegated cream to light brown, cream and white stitching is worked on a dull green background. To give a heavy, raised effect, a padding of threads is laid under the bars, which are then worked over with close stem stitches.

Portuguese border
Stem stitch over bars. Each band of stitches must be worked separately, starting at the base with the left hand side, then the right hand side

Portuguese border *page 129*
Stem stitch is worked on bars again but must start at the base of these, working upwards; the left hand rows are worked separately from those on the right hand side of the bars, to give the V shape in the centre between the stitches.
A variety of yarns is used for this sampler, including weaving yarn, perle cotton numbers 5 and 8 sewing cotton, gimp, slub cotton
The background is blue with white and cream stitches

Portuguese border

126

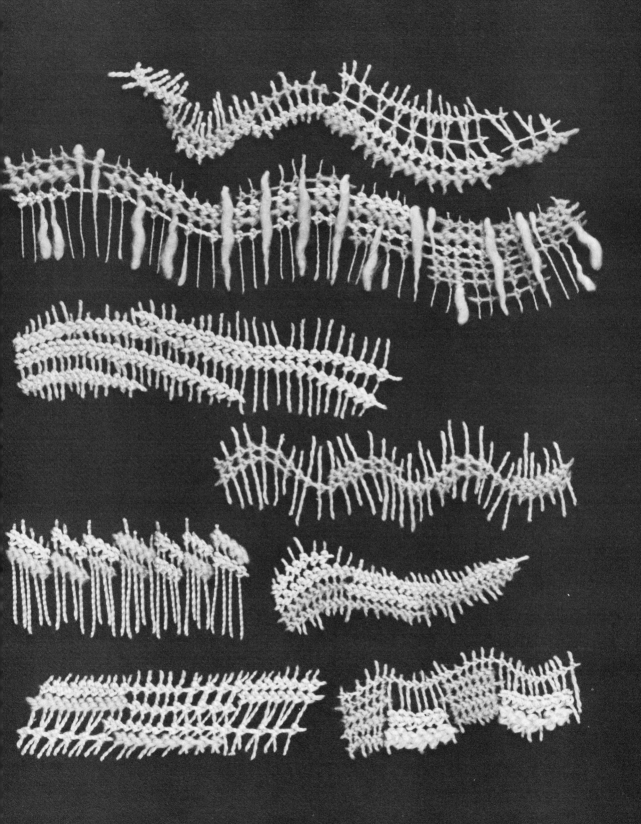

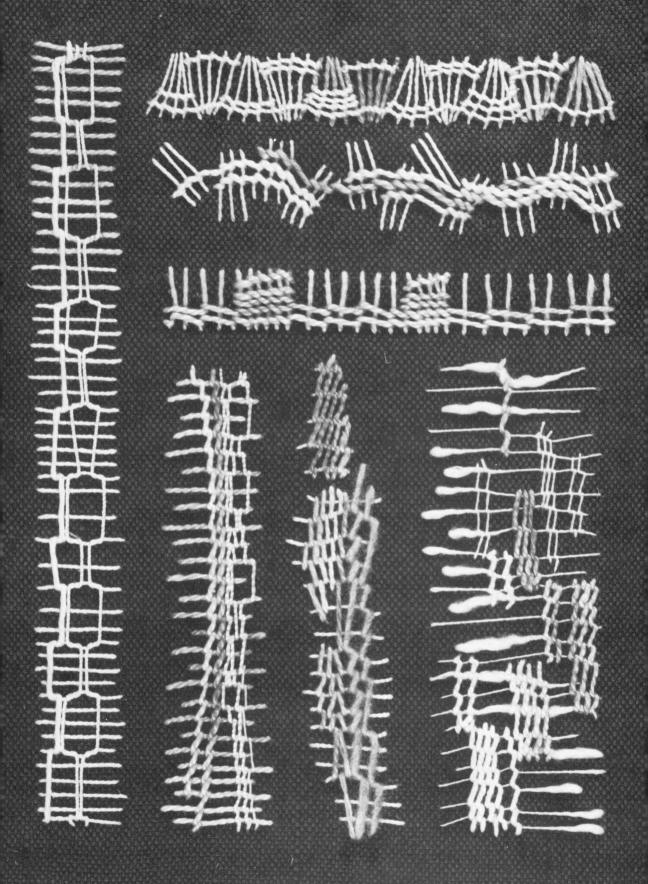

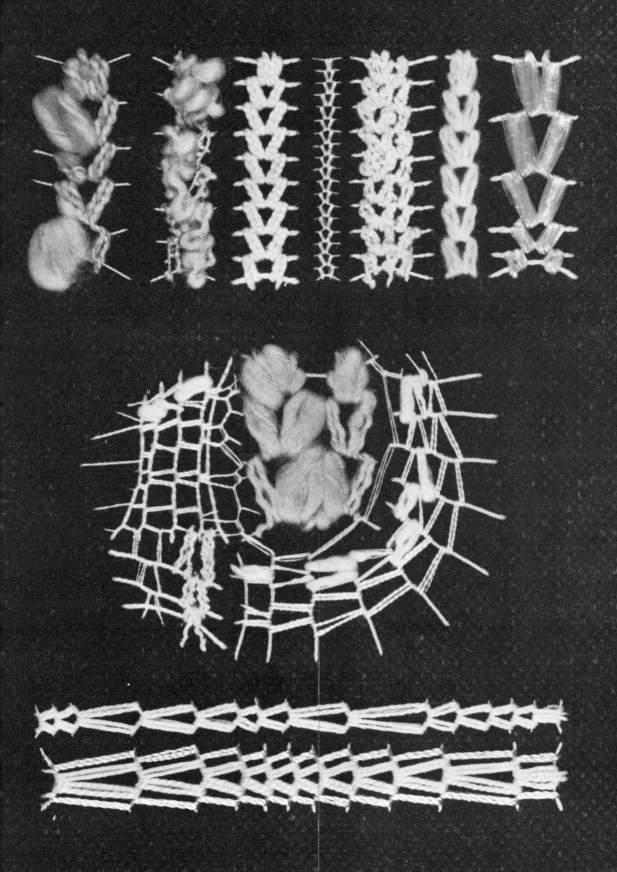

Satin stitch   *opposite*

Satin stitch gives a smooth band, is worked from left to right, vertically or diagonally, or horizontally. The direction in which the stitch lies gives strong tonal contrast

This sampler shows blocks of satin stitch arranged at different angles to catch the light. Stranded cottons using 1 to 6 threads, perle cotton numbers 5 and 8, coton-a-broder numbers 6 and 16, rayon twist weaving yarn and fine crochet cotton are used for the stitches, in white and creams on a brown background

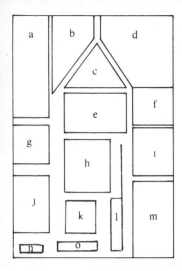

Stitches on hexagonal net

Arranged to form a house with a garden. The variety of patterns obtainable is infinite and sufficiently interesting worked in white on white net. Colour could ruin the unity of the sampler with its open and close textural patterns.

(a) Straight stitch
(b) Satin stitch
(c) Honeycomb filling
(d) Cross with guilloche movement
(e) Wave filling worked from the back
(f) Satin
(g) Counted satin
(h) Buttonhole stitch, two in one hole
(i) Wave filling
(j) Straight florentine
(k) Counted satin with darned edge
(l) Counted satin
(m) Wave filling
(n) Eyelets
(o) Stem stitch and velvet loops

Detached loop stitch

Structurally similar to twisted chain. It is detached and stands away from the fabric

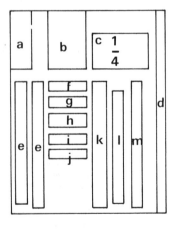

Detached loop stitch and variations
and Sorbello variations   *opposite*

The stitches are in variegated yarns, cream to white and white on scarlet cotton.

A number of different threads are used including varigated yarn, perle cottons numbers 3, 5 and 8, crochet cotton wool, weaving yarns, soft cotton

(a)   Loop stitch in slub cotton
(b)   Loop stitch in variegated yarn, tied and dyed
(c)   1 Sorbello in perle cotton number 8. Variation worked from the right in the illustration
      2 Double knot stitch in tied and dyed yarn
      3 Sorbello worked from the left, variation in tied and dyed yarn
      4 Sorbello variation, worked from the right in crochet cotton
(d)   Loop stitch in wools and perle cotton number 3
(e)   Sorbello variations in tied and dyed weaving yarn and soft cotton
(f)   Loop stitch in variegated yarn
(g)   Sorbello or double knot variation
(h)   Loop stitch in weaving yarn
(i)   Sorbello in weaving yarn
(j)   Loop stitch in tied and dyed weaving yarn
(k)   Sorbello variation in soft cotton
(l)   Similar variation in tied and dyed yarn

Suppliers in Great Britain

Embroidery threads and accessories

Mary Allen
Turnditch, Derbyshire

E J Arnold and Son Limited
(School Suppliers)
Butterley Street
Leeds LS10 1AX

Art Needlework Industries
Limited
7 St Michael's Mansions
Ship Street
Oxford OX1 3DG

The Campden Needlecraft
Centre
High Street
Chipping Campden
Gloucestershire

Craftsman's Mark Limited
Broadlands, Shortheath
Farnham, Surrey

de Denne Ltd
159–161 Kenton Road
Kenton
Harrow
Middlesex

Dryad (Reeves) Limited
Northgates
Leicester LE1 4QR

B Francis
4 Glenworth Street
London NW1

Fresew
97 The Paddocks
Stevenage
Herts SG2 9UQ

Louis Grossé Limited
36 Manchester Street
London W1 5PE

Handweavers Studio
29 Haroldstone Road
Walthamstow
London E17 7AN

The Handworkers' Market
8 Fish Hill
Holt, Norfolk

Harrods Limited
London SW1

Ruth John
30 Hunts Pond Road
Park Gate
Southampton

Levencrafts
54 Church Square
Guisborough, Cleveland

Mace and Nairn
89 Crane Street
Salisbury, Wiltshire SP1 2PY

MacCulloch and Wallis
Limited
25–26 Dering Street
London W1R 0BH

The Needlecraft Shop
corner Smallgate/Station Road
Beccles
Suffolk

Nottingham Handcraft
Company (School Suppliers)
Melton Road
West Bridgford
Nottingham

Christine Riley
53 Barclay Street
Stonehaven
Kincardineshire AB3 2AR

Royal School of Needlework
25 Princes Gate
Kensington SW7 1QE

The Silver Thimble
33 Gay Street
Bath

J Henry Smith Limited
Park Road, Calverton
Woodborough
nr Nottingham

Mrs Joan L Trickett
110 Marsden Road
Burnley, Lancashire

Suppliers in the USA

Embroidery threads and accessories

Appleton Brothers of London
West Main Road
Little Compton
Rhode Island 02837

American Crewel Studio
Box 298 Boonton
New Jersey 07005

American Thread
Corporation
90 Park Avenue
New York

Bucky King Embroideries
Unlimited,
Box 371, King Bros
3 Ranch, Buffalo Star Rte
Sheriden
Wyoming 82801

Casa de las Tejedoras
1618 East Edinger
Santa Ana
California 92705

Craft Kaleidoscope
6412 Ferguson Street
Indianapolis 46220

Dharma Trading Company
1952 University Avenue
Berkeley
California 94704

Folklorico Yarn Co
522 Ramona Street
Palo Alto 94301
California

The Golden Eye
Box 205
Chestnut Hill
Massachusetts 02167

Head and Tails
River Forest
Illinois 60305

Leonida Leatherdale
Embroidery Studio
90 East Gate
Winnipeg,
Manitoba R3C 2C3
Canada

Lily Mills
Shelby
North Carolina 28150

The Needle's Point Studio
216 Appleblossom Court
Vienna
Virginia 22180

Sutton Yarns
2054 Yonge Street
Toronto 315
Ontario, Canada

Threadbenders
2260 Como Avenue
St Paul, Minnesota 55108

The Thread Shed
307 Freeport Road
Pittsburgh
Pennsylvania 15215

Yarn Bazaar
Yarncrafts Limited
3146 M Street
North West Washington DC

Yarn Depot
545 Sutter Street
San Francisco 94118
California

Index to stitches

The numbers in *italics* refer to photographs

Arrow or arrowhead 22, *23*

Back 12, 14, *15*, 18, *21*, 22, 24, 31
Back and running 12, 14, *15*
Blanket or buttonhole 10, 11, 40, *41*, 42 45
Blanket, closed 42, *43*
Blanket, crossed 42, *43*
Bonnet 56, *57*
Broad chain 110
Bullion knots 114, *116*, *117*, *colour plate 3*
  looped 114, *116*
  with tails 114
  without tails 114
Buttonhole 40, *41*, 54, *55*
  on hexagonal net 132, *133*
Buttonhole, closed 42, *44*
  detached 54, *55*
  knotted 52, *53*
  loops 32, 42
  up-and-down 42, *43*, 48, *49*, 50, *51*, 54, *55*
  wrapped 54, *55*
Buttonhole over detached threads 54, *55*
Buttonhole variations 42, *45*

Cable chain 98, 106
  easy 98
  knotted 106, *107*
    variations 102, *103*
Chain 88, *89*
  broad 110
  detached 88, *90*, *91*, 118, *119*
  double 98, *99*, *100*, 106, *107*
    variations 98, *100*
    with buttonhole 106
  heavy 108, *109*
  open 54, *55*, 102, 108
    variations 110
  raised band *frontispiece, colour plate 4*, 126, *127*, *129*
  rosette 104, *105*
  solid filling 110
  square (or open) 108, *109*
  twisted 76, 82, *83*, 92, *94*, 96, *97*, 104
  wrapped 31
  zigzag 54, *55*, 92, *93*, 106, *107*, 118, *119*
    variations 92, *93*
Chevron 78, *79*, 80, 118, *119*
Chinest knot 114, *115*

Closed blanket 42, *44*
Closed buttonhole 42, *44*
Coral or twisted chain 96, *97*
Coral knot 92
Coral zigzag 92, *94*, *95*, 120, *121*
Couching 118, *119*
  looped
    Roumanian 118, *119*, 120, 122, *123*
    with buttonhole 120, *121*
    with feather 120, *121*
    with fly 120, *121*
    with herringbone 120, *121*
    with zigzag coral 120, *121*
Cretan *frontispiece*, 54, *55*, 82, *83*, 118, *119*
Cretan and variations 82, *83*, *84*, *85*
Cross 24, *25*
  threaded 114
  with guilloche movement on hexagonal net 132, *133*
Crossed blanket 42

Darning, Japanese 14, *17*
Detached chain *frontispiece, colour plate 3*
Detached loops 134, *135*
  variations 134, *135*
Double chain 98, *99*
  variations 98, *100*
Double knot or Palestrina 32, *33*, *34*, *35*
  variations 32, 38
  and closed herringbone variations 38
  with buttonhole 38, *39*

Easy cable chain 106, *107*
Eyelets on hexagonal net 132, *133*

Feather 58, *59*
Fly *frontispiece*, 58, 60, *61*
  knotted 62, *63*
  twisted 62, *63*
  variations 62, *63*
  with buttonhole 62, *63*
French knots *frontispiece*, 114, *115*

German interlacing 71, *72*

Half Portuguese stem 28, *29*, 30
Heavy chain 108, *109*
Herringbone 14, *17*, 68, *69*, 71, *72*
  closed 68, *69*, 74, *75*
    with chain 74, *75*
    with double knot 34, *35*
    with twisted chain 38, *39*, 74, *75*
      variations 38

knotted 76
open twisted 74, *75*
twisted 74, *75*
variations 68
Herringbone and closed herringbone 68
Herringbone pile 74, *75*
Honeycomb filling on hexagonal net
132, *133*

Interlaced herringbone 71, *72*
Interlaced square 71, *73*
Interlacing, German 71, *72*
Invented stitches based on
  herringbone 77
    tied 106, *107*
    with twisted chain 76
      surrounded with chain 76
    sorbello with twisted chain 34, *35*
    stem with buttonhole 30, *31*
    with wrapped chain 31

Japanese darning 14, *17*

Knot, double 32, *33*, 34, *35*
  threaded
  variations 32, 38
  with buttonhole 38, *39*
Knotted cable chain 106, *107*
  variations 102, *103*

Loop 34, *35*, 42, *43*, 135, *135*
Loops, detached 134, *135*
  variations 134, *135*

Maltese 71, *72*

Needleweaving 40, *41*, 54, *55*
  on detached threads

Open chain 102, *108*
  variations
Outline 24

Palestrina or double knot 32, *33*
Pekinese 18, *21*
Porguguese border 126

Raised chain band *frontispiece, colour
  plate 4*, 126, *127*, *129*
Raised stem band 28, *29*
Rosette chain 104, *105*
Roumanian couching *colour plate 3*, 120,
  121
  over two threads *colour plate 3*, 120,
    121
Running *frontispiece*, 12, *13*, 14, *15*
  and darning 14

back and 14, *15*
leaving loops 12, *13*
random 12, *13*
threaded 18, *19*, *20*
Running on couched thread 12, *13*

Satin *frontispiece*, 110, 118, *119*
  counted on hexagonal net 132, *133*
Seeding (or Speckling) *frontispiece*, 12
Sheaf 64, *65*, 66, *67*
Solid fillings on hexagonal net
  chain 110
    open 110
    satin 130, *131*
    stem 110
Sorbello 32, 34, 36, 134, *135*
  variations 36, *37*, 134, *135*
Speckling (or Seeding) *frontispiece*, 12
Square chain (or open) 108, 109
Star 14, *17*
Stem 24, *26*, 30, *31*, 110, *colour plate 2*
  band raised 28, *29*
  elongated 28, *29*
  half Portuguese 28, *29*, 30
  slanting 24
  wrapped 28, *29*
  variations 28, *29*, 30, *31*
Stem with bullion on twisted chain
  with buttonhole and chain 28, *29*
  with chain at side 28, *29*
  with horizontal blanket or loop 34, *35*
  with thread behind needle 30
  with twisted chain 31, 34, *35*
  with twisted chain and chain 31
Straight 22, *23*, 86, 110, *colour plate 1*
  on hexagonal net 132, *133*
Straight Florentine on hexagonal net
  132, *133*

Thorn 124, *125*
  easy method 124
  usual method 124
Threaded crosses 114
Threaded running 18, *19*, *20*
Twisted chain 30, 31
  variation 31
Twisted fly 62, *63*

Up and down buttonhole 42, *43*, 48, *49*,
  50, *51*, 54, *55*
  variations 48, *51*

Wave 86, *87*
  filling on hexagonal net 132, *133*
Wheatear *frontispiece*, 110, *111*, *112*, *113*

Zigzag chain 54
  coral 92, *94*, *95*, 120, *121*